T0266670

"Becca Powers gets it right. The journey ⌣ ---- ⌣ _
by leading with your unique strengths and talents in a way that
generates positive outcomes and gives others permission to do the
same. Her book is the step-by-step guide to do just that."
— **Howard Behar**, former president, Starbucks Coffee

"This potent and practical gem of a book is a compass guiding you
on the most sacred journey you'll ever take — the journey to truly
owning your worth."
— **Nancy Levin**, author of *Worthy* and *Setting Boundaries Will Set
You Free* and founder of Levin Life Coach Academy

"For anyone seeking to live a more vibrant and authentic life, this
book is a revelation, offering practical tools and insights to discover
the transformative power of your inner radiance."
— **Siri Lindley**, two-time world-champion triathlete,
Tony Robbins speaker, and author of *Finding a Way*

"*A Return to Radiance* is a much-needed hands-on guide through the
often-rocky terrain of business, self-worth, and spiritual and material actualization. Becca Powers, creator of the lauded POWER
Method, invites readers to sip from her deep reservoir of knowledge
and offers specific steps toward fulfillment. She channels the generous spirit of spiritual thinking pioneers like Shakti Gawain along
with the business acumen of Adam Grant to help you unlock abundance and manifest the limitless potential in your career — and
life. This book is soul food, lighting the way toward confidence and
prosperity for today's professionals."
— **Estelle Erasmus**, author of *Writing That Gets Noticed:
Find Your Voice, Become a Better Storyteller, Get Published*,
NYU writing professor, and contributing editor at *Writer's Digest*

"*A Return to Radiance* is your ticket to unlocking the best version
of yourself. Becca Powers's powerful guidance will empower you to

break free from limiting beliefs and tap into your inner reservoir of potential, leading to a life of balance, harmony, and limitless possibility. Get ready to shine bright and make a positive impact in the world!"

— **Bill Philipps,** psychic medium and author of *Expect the Unexpected, Signs from the Other Side,* and *Soul Searching*

"A Return to Radiance is a beautiful reminder that all we have to do is return to our radiance, that it never went anywhere. By sharing personal stories, case studies, actionable steps, and deep insight into how to tap into our own wellness and knowing, Becca Powers takes the reader on a journey of rediscovery and reenforcement of our already present love of self and potential."

— **Tricia Brouk,** international award-winning director, author, producer, and founder of the Big Talk Academy

"With *A Return to Radiance,* Becca Powers proves herself to be not just an author but a visionary in the realm of personal development. She adeptly blends wisdom, empathy, and practical strategies to guide readers on a journey of self-discovery and empowerment. This book is a brilliant light in the pursuit of understanding one's true self and living a life that truly shines."

— **Jessie Andres,** regional sales manager, ExtraHop

"This exciting and inspiring guide will jump-start your dreams into reality. Becca Powers is your superpower whisperer. With heart and a wealth of inviting tools, Powers coaches and cheers you as you learn to uproot the habits that drain your energy and choose for your inherent spark and glow."

— **Meredith Heller,** author of *Writing by Heart* and *Write a Poem, Save Your Life*

"Becca Powers's *A Return to Radiance* is a transformative journey that compels readers to explore the depths of their potential and unleash their inner brilliance. With a mix of personal anecdotes, practical exercises, and profound insights, Powers invites us to break free from the confines of burnout and embrace a life of purpose, joy, and fulfillment. Her POWER Method is a masterful blend of science, psychology, and spirituality that's clear, practical, and empowering. This book is a must-read for anyone seeking to ignite their soul, elevate their energy, and live a life that resonates with authenticity and radiance."

— **Aria Johnson**, TV personality and keynote speaker,
Behind the Glitz

"In a world where our unique brilliance often lies dormant, Becca Powers invites us to embrace our creativity, build deeper connections, and rediscover our passions and purpose. *A Return to Radiance* is a thought-provoking, beautiful book that takes readers on a soulful journey they may not have known they needed."

— **Kate Volman**, CEO, Floyd Coaching

"*A Return to Radiance* is the professional and personal life manual you have been waiting for. Becca Powers gives you the tools to evaluate all areas of yourself and your life. She provides proven strategies and techniques for showing up for yourself, leveling up, and taking action while bringing you on a journey and providing real-life lessons to get the most out of this one life! This is a one-stop resource for connecting your personal, professional, physical, spiritual, and emotional selves to achieve your purpose, passion, and potential!"

— **Connie Woolsey**, vice president of retail operations,
Cresco Labs

"*A Return to Radiance* by Becca Powers is not just a book; it's an experience. Becca has done the hard work herself. Her experiences in her own self-discovery and empowerment have put her in a position to chart an easy-to-navigate path for your journey. Thank you, Becca, for removing the hurdles and providing a practical way forward for those of us who don't know where to start in identifying and igniting our individual inner light."

— **Gina McCarthy**, enterprise account executive,
Abnormal Security

"Becca Powers has crafted a masterful guide to finding one's true essence and living a life of purpose and passion. Through *A Return to Radiance*, she offers a beacon of hope and a practical road map for anyone seeking to uncover their innate brilliance. Her compelling narrative and actionable advice make this book an essential resource for personal transformation."

— **Erin Wirth**, enterprise account executive, Dynatrace

A RETURN
TO
Radiance

A RETURN TO *Radiance*

The POWER Method to Ignite Your Soul and Unleash Your Potential

BECCA POWERS

New World Library
Novato, California

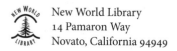

New World Library
14 Pamaron Way
Novato, California 94949

Text design by Tona Pearce Myers

Library of Congress Cataloging-in-Publication Data

Names: Powers, Becca, author.
Title: A return to radiance : the power method to ignite your soul and unleash your potential / Becca Powers.
Description: Novato, California : New World Library, [2024] | Includes bibliographical references. | Summary: "*A Return to Radiance* gives today's working men and women the tools to reclaim brilliance, overcome obstacles, grow resilience, banish impostor syndrome, and craft a life that leaves a legacy of empowerment"-- Provided by publisher.
Identifiers: LCCN 2024026004 (print) | LCCN 2024026005 (ebook) | ISBN 9781608689347 (paperback) | ISBN 9781608689354 (epub)
Subjects: LCSH: Self-realization. | Self-actualization (Psychology) | Success.
Classification: LCC BF637.S4 P694 2024 (print) | LCC BF637.S4 (ebook) | DDC 158.1--dc23/eng/20240701
LC record available at https://lccn.loc.gov/2024026004
LC ebook record available at https://lccn.loc.gov/2024026005

First printing, October 2024
ISBN 978-1-60868-934-7
Ebook ISBN 978-1-60868-935-4
Printed in Canada

10   9   8   7   6   5   4   3   2   1

New World Library is committed to protecting our natural environment. This book is made of material from well-managed FSC®-certified forests and other controlled sources.

This book is dedicated to my mom, Gail, and my dad, Bob. Thank you for living in your radiance and showing me the importance of never dimming your light. Your legacy carries on through me with every word I write.

Contents

Part 4: Elevate Your Energy

Part 5: Rock Your Radiance

Foreword

*H*ave you ever been in the presence of someone who radiates passion and purpose in everything they do? Have you watched someone in action who is deeply committed to their calling? Or better yet, have you ever personally witnessed someone who has turned their pain into power and is on a mission to leave this world better than they found it?

Well, Becca Powers is the epitome of a resilient leader, speaker, and transformational trainer for ambitious individuals and corporate teams who are ready to shed the status quo, seek alignment in their personal and professional lives, and give themselves permission to create abundant possibilities for their futures. I can guarantee she is going to do that for you, too!

I've had the honor of running, not walking, alongside Becca for the past few years as her business coach and, most importantly, as a member of her fan club of supporters who adore her. I love and value being part of someone's journey who is so fiercely committed to making the most out of life and who treats their calling to impact others as a spiritual assignment to make a massive difference in this world. From the moment we first connected, I knew she was special and that I had to be part of "Team Becca." I could literally *feel* her passion and energy through the phone as she shared how she has simultaneously dominated the leaderboards in her sales career while also pursuing writing, entrepreneurship, and public speaking.

Her multidimensional life and pursuits are all centered around helping people step into their purpose and power and, most importantly, align their radiant selves with where they're headed, not just where they've been. Because Becca encourages and embraces every facet of the individuals she inspires and trains, her impact is profound and refreshing. Simply stated: She's been called to do this work and is in a beautiful position to do so.

There's no better person than Becca to learn from when it comes to reconnecting with yourself. Her fresh perspective and approach allow her spiritual prowess and personal development expertise to merge, providing a unique perspective that you'll appreciate. In true Becca fashion, she creates space and holds up a mirror in order for you to evaluate where you are versus where you want to be. Most importantly, she helps you define *who* you want to be and how you want to show up in this world as your most empowered self. Because she's results driven, she also gives you what you need to make moves, create better alignment, and equip yourself with resources to help you truly step into your power.

Becca's vulnerability and authenticity shine through as she shares lived experiences intended to help you reconnect to yourself. Her radiant light beams through every page of this book, which is written as though she's a familiar friend who wants the best for you and who is willing to walk alongside you to help figure out the next steps on your journey of life. She intentionally, yet gently, creates the space for self-reflection, the guidance needed to pivot and realign to your purpose, and gives you the boost you need to chase after your dreams, even if you feel as though you've neglected them for longer than you should have.

Becca's guidance is laced with stories filled with so many relatable experiences, which only one who has walked the walk and talked the talk can share. What I adore about Becca and this book is that she unapologetically sheds the perception that success comes easily. As a Fortune 500 sales leader who has a parallel path as an influential consultant and speaker, Becca weaves countless examples from her personal and professional life throughout the book to showcase how you, too, can truly be who you are and why you must show up fully as yourself to live a happy, purposeful, and fulfilled life.

Becca herself is a beautiful blend of corporate badass and entrepreneur. She challenges herself each and every day to be her best while never allowing her true light to dim. Has this come easily? No, but she's continued to stay committed to her truth and shares with you throughout every page how you can do this, too. Becca was called to do this work and will help you uncover your calling as well.

How liberating will it be to stand in your truth, shine brightly, and embrace who you are? I'm sure it will be life-changing, and I guarantee you'll be much closer to doing so as you enjoy this book and put her advice into motion. Consider this your compass to help you come back to yourself, break from the mundane, reignite your passion for who you are and what you do, and give yourself permission to evolve into the person you were meant to be. Get ready to experience your own transformation as you reclaim your radiance and your joy. I'm so excited for you and will be cheering you on every step of the way!

Allison Walsh
Founder of Allison Walsh Consulting
and bestselling author of *She Believed She Could:*
Show Up, Shine Bright, and Achieve Abundant Success

Introduction

The room was dimly lit. There was a haze in the air from all the cigarette smoke. The stage lights glistened in a multicolored shimmer as they pierced through the fog of the bar. The atmosphere contained a sense of magic and connection as the audience joyfully sang along to the band's every lyric.

That was nothing compared to the radiant glow beaming from the lead guitar player as the spotlight shone on him — highlighting the epic solo that was about to go down. Bob leaned into his guitar with the ease and grace of someone expressing their natural-born talent.

Bob closed his eyes as he played the first few chords of the legendary guitar solo from Pink Floyd's "Comfortably Numb." The moment his fingers hit those strings, the energy of the room shifted to awe. The crowd knew every exact note, and for a split second, I could tell they were questioning whether he was going to be able to pull this off.

One might feel extreme pressure with such high expectations, but not Bob. The audience wanted him to deliver the music they knew and loved, and he was clearly in a mystical zone of genius as he flawlessly and effortlessly crushed the performance note for note, with eyes closed.

I could see that Bob felt the music; he didn't think the music. He wasn't playing that guitar solo; the guitar solo was playing through Bob. It was as if some invisible force had taken over his fingers. A few men in the bar rose to their feet to play their own air guitar solo. Others had tears in their eyes as the song awakened personal emotions and memories. Everyone was feeling the magic that Bob was radiating from the depths of his soul. Bob was a bridge of cosmic connection between the Universe and the folks in that bar.

As the solo came to an end, Bob belted out the lyrics, eyes still closed. He wasn't just the band's guitar player — he was also the lead singer. The crowd sang along with the same passion and zest, matching the band's performance. The song finished and everyone stood to clap and holler — loving every ounce of the performance.

The energy was electrifying. My mom reached over and grabbed my hand, made eye contact with me, and gave me a huge smile. My seven-year-old self had just witnessed this man move an entire audience into a standing ovation. I looked back at my mom beaming in pride — that man on stage was my dad.

The Spark Inside

Have you ever noticed something special about someone? Can you recall what made them stand out — was it their energy, their talent, their zest for life?

Something intangible made a deep impression on you. Perhaps you got goose bumps or butterflies in your stomach. Maybe they elicited love, laughter, or inspiration. What you witnessed was the spark inside them. The part of them that is limitless and budding with potential. And you, fierce one, have that spark inside you, too. All of us do.

That spark inside can open the doors to the ultimate manifestation of your success, happiness, health, wealth, and fulfillment — so if you could, wouldn't you choose to nurture it? I am sure we all would!

This book is your invitation to do just that — to nurture your spark and return to your radiance. On this journey, consider me your awakening agent. I'm here to help you remember how magnificent you are. I intend this book to serve as your trusty guide showing you how to embrace all that you are, one step at a time.

This journey is of utmost importance and will change your life in the most magical and unexpected ways. I believe that we are all born with unique gifts, talents, and strengths bestowed upon us. It's our job to reveal what they are and rise into our peak potential.

The truth is that you are made of the same elements as the cosmos and are just as boundless. Imagine that this spark inside connects you with infinite possibilities and to your inner genius. These timeless parts of ourselves know how to solve problems faster, create with clarity, work on our strengths and talents with confidence, and live life from a place of self-assurance knowing that life is happening for us. What would happen if you truly believed this? Anything would be possible — and it is!

Witnessing my dad on stage in front of a live audience as he played the guitar as if it were a true extension of his soul was the first time I recall seeing someone's radiance. I immediately understood that we all possess a specialness. This spark inside us — like an electric current — when we are in sync with the fullness of our potential and expressing it is awe-inspiring. It leaves a lasting impact on others and fills us with joy, fulfillment, and liberation.

The Radiant Self

Picture having a superpower hidden within you that has been there all along — that's your radiance. Much like your favorite superhero, you have a unique gift that when unleashed changes the world for the better. But where is it and how do you access it?

Our radiance is both within us and in the energy that surrounds us. On average, our radiant field encapsulates the first eighteen to thirty-six inches around our body. For example, if we were to stick our arm straight out in front of us, our radiant field would range from the tip of our fingers back to our shoulder.

Our energy levels determine how easy it is to access the gifts within our radiant field. When our energy is high, our radiant field expands, making it easier to tap into our potential. When our energy is low, our radiant field withdraws closer to our body, making it much harder to do things with ease, let alone access all the magnificence that we truly are.

Returning to our radiance isn't just about uncovering our gifts and talents and letting them loose in the world. It's about infusing them into every nook and cranny of our lives, from how we rock our day-to-day grind to how we navigate love and leadership. Imagine being like Bob, belting out the epic guitar solo of your soul, not just in those fleeting moments of cosmic connection, but in everything you do.

Your radiance is your soul's fireworks in this human journey. In it lie your unique superpowers. It's the truth of who you are and what you're here for. Your dreams, potential, purpose, and power to rock this world in unimaginable ways exist within it. Everyone is born with this radiance; it's our birthright to express it in a grand finale display that is so awe-inspiring it lights up the night sky.

The POWER Method

Have you ever wanted to create change? Or unapologetically chase your dreams? Yet for some reason you stop before you ever get started? The task, as inspiring as it may be, just feels so daunting that it's easier to settle — to stay the same. If this sounds like you, you are not alone.

The biggest problem that prevents people from chasing their dreams and making changes is not knowing how to do it. Most people are capable and able to create change as long as they have the willingness and confidence to do so.

The POWER Method exists because there was a time when

I needed a how-to manual. Several years ago, I was way out of alignment with my true self and my full potential. I was powering through my days, pretending that my dreams didn't matter, that it was selfish to prioritize my well-being and my desires. I had forgotten what radiance even was. It was as if I had never even seen it before. Until I burned out.

I was nearly hospitalized from extreme fatigue and crippling anxiety. My burnout left a trail of disarray behind me. My marriage was on the edge of divorce, my relationships with my kids were disconnected, and debt was piling up. I was a mere shadow of myself.

Everything looked perfect on the outside, but I was falling apart on the inside. I was a successful senior sales leader at one of the award-winning Fortune 100's best companies to work for, a wife to a firefighter, a mom to a blended family of four kids, and the owner of a house on a lake with a fence and two dogs. When I hit the peak of what I call my UN-potential, life felt incredibly hard and unmanageable. I was desperate for change; I could feel my life slipping through my fingertips.

It took me a few years to turn my life around to where it is now. Thankfully, there were things I was able to implement immediately that began to rewrite my story — and I will share these. If you have ever felt depleted and disconnected from yourself, know that the journey to becoming all that you were born to be and returning to your radiance takes time, patience, and commitment. Be nice to yourself because, on the other side of this work, your best life is waiting for you.

The POWER Method is a combination of science, psychology, and metaphysics that aligns you with the fullness of your potential — and gets you there fast! I have dedicated hundreds of hours to achieving certifications, including becoming a high-performance trainer, Kundalini yoga teacher (levels one and two), and executive life coach with a specialization in limited beliefs and trauma awareness. I have invested more than six figures trying to learn the magical how-tos, not only to heal but to live a life that mirrors the brilliance that exists inside.

This journey of self-discovery has lasted years, going from daily meditations to retreats to deep reflection to eventually doing the work that transformed my life. After turning around my life and career — saving my marriage, cultivating deep and loving relationships with the people I care about, sustaining my success and well-being, and relishing in the gifts of my radiance — I felt confident that I had discovered a best-of framework that would help other people do the same.

I began to coach careered individuals with my method, and it worked for them, too. They started to see six-figure commission checks, sparks in their creativity, two-level promotions, new businesses, and breakthroughs in their mental and emotional health. This led to referrals for corporate trainings to help teams and employees elevate their impact and improve their performance. I have the honor of working with some of the largest organizations in the world, like Dell, Cisco, and Royal Caribbean, and I have shared with them this proven framework to prevent burnout, align people with their strengths, improve team collaboration, generate sky-rocketing results, and so much more.

The POWER Method is my proprietary method for helping you become everything you are meant to be. It can help you unleash your potential and serve as your how-to manual. This framework has five pillars that form the acronym POWER, and these match the five parts of this book:

- Protect your potential
- Own your opportunities
- Waken your worthiness
- Elevate your energy
- Rock your radiance

THE POWER *Method*

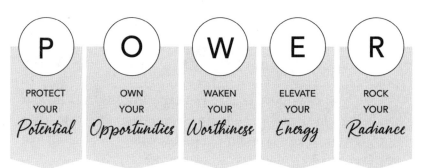

P — PROTECT YOUR *Potential*

O — OWN YOUR *Opportunities*

W — WAKEN YOUR *Worthiness*

E — ELEVATE YOUR *Energy*

R — ROCK YOUR *Radiance*

Radiant Resources

Each chapter is packed with messages, lessons, tools, and techniques to explore. At the end of each chapter, the "POWER Up Your Practice" section provides an exercise to support your transformation. The chapters also end with the section "Grab Your Gemstone," which summarizes the chapter's core theme, and a "POWER Thought" to empower you along your journey. As you read each chapter, you might encounter new concepts that resonate deeply, sparking a desire to dive even deeper, and others may not sparkle for you the same way. I encourage you to be open to the process because sometimes getting out of our comfort zone is the very thing that leads to a breakthrough. Think of yourself as an explorer on a self-actualization expedition, and your job is to figure out which tools unearth the discovery underneath the surface.

My goal is to be your trusted guide and make your return-to-radiance journey as transformative as possible. To enhance your experience, you can download the complimentary Return to Radiance Personal Transformation Guide, which is packed with

all the POWER Up Your Practice exercises and more, at Resources
.ReturnToRadianceBook.com.

    The level of positive change you experience is truly in your
hands. Personal transformation is a lifetime commitment to never
stop growing. It also takes time. Take baby steps or go all-in, but
whatever you do — don't stay where you are.

    Your radiance awaits!

PART ONE

PROTECT YOUR
Potential

The only limits to the possibilities
in your life tomorrow are the "buts" you use today.

— Les Brown

CHAPTER ONE

Break Up with Burnout

*I*f you had to guess, what percentage of working professionals do you think are suffering from or on the verge of burnout? According to a 2022 survey of eight thousand people conducted by my company, Powers Peak Potential, 69 percent of respondents reported being burned out and another 29 percent reported showing signs and symptoms of burnout. That means only 2 percent of respondents, or 160 people, were reported to be fully thriving.

We are living and working in a time when it is more common to be burned out than it is to be living our best lives. When I think of what it takes to reconnect with those limitless and cosmic parts of ourselves, the very first thing I think of is how necessary it is to learn how to break up with burnout.

When the Music Stopped

When I was born, both my parents were full-time musicians. I grew up in an environment where people freely and proudly displayed their gifts, talents, and strengths — as if it was the most natural thing to do. I saw people unapologetically lean into their awesomeness. At a young age, I had a profound understanding that there is something brilliant about every single one of us and we are born to express it.

Unknown to me at that time, I soon learned another side of this truth. Burning brightly also requires us to protect our potential or we run the risk of our flame burning out. By the time I got to high school, my homelife was much different. Work, bills, kids, and responsibility took center stage over my parents' music. Their efforts to have a career and also a musical calling were causing conflicts. The more distance they felt from their musical abilities, and the less space they had to express them, the more depressed they became. It was as if they were becoming disconnected from their souls' cosmic connection and they knew it.

What happened next is the catalyst behind why this work of rising to the fullness of our potential is so important. The music stopped. Literally and figuratively. Both my mom and my dad passed away separately from a losing battle with deep depression. My mom was forty-six and my dad was sixty-two when it happened. Being that my parents were made up of peace, love, and happiness *and* sex, drugs, and rock and roll, I chalked up their early transitions to reckless self-neglect.

There may be some truth to that because burnout does happen because of self-neglect. I had my run-in with extreme burnout and learned this to be true. Now I also know that there is more to the story than just intentional or unintentional self-neglect.

My story is different from my parents', yet it has similar markings — and yours may, too. While I'm not a musician, I understand the passion and love my parents had for creating and expressing what was alive and burning inside them. I have always been a businesswoman, and my passions have been in communication, like building relationships, creating concepts, writing, speaking, training, and so on. A career in sales has always been a perfect fit for me — until the day it wasn't.

In 2014, I was working in a toxic work environment as a senior sales leader while trying to raise four kids in middle school. During this period, my dad unexpectedly passed away, which triggered the unresolved grief of my mom's passing years earlier.

It felt like a hurricane was swirling inside me. Instead of preparing for the storm, I continued on my charter forward. For three years, I ignored the red flags, powered through the turbulent days, and ignored the warning signs that my system — my mind, body, and soul — was overloaded. When the storm finally got the best of me, I was running on empty. I was disconnected from my soul, my passions, my family, and myself.

I realized that what was happening to me was very similar to what happened to my parents. I, too, was depressed. Bills, work, kids, and responsibilities took the lead over my well-being. Coming to terms with the fact that I was headed down the same road as my parents forced me to protect my well-being from the catastrophic destruction of this hurricane inside. During this time, I began to find ways to protect my potential, which was something my parents had been unable to do. I was bound and determined to turn things around, stay in my career field, and redefine what was possible.

To do this, I had to turn my attention inward. This led to deep reflection and major shifts in perception. In this space, the most profound thought emerged. My parents did not pass away from reckless neglect. They passed away because they were disconnected from their souls and because they didn't know how to nurture their radiance. I believe that if they had found a way to have a career and express themselves as talented musicians without sacrificing their well-being — they would still be alive today.

Here's the good news for you! You get to nurture and cultivate your radiance. Your career and calling are your own. They might be similar to mine or my parents', or they might be entirely different. Either way, if you are tapped into your radiance and expressing your gifts, you will experience success, happiness, well-being, and fulfillment. So much so that it sets your soul on fire.

Understanding Burnout

Burnout is the archnemesis of personal growth and is often the main culprit that prevents us from rocking our radiance. Burnout keeps us stuck in our UN-potential. As I became an expert in peak potential, I also became an expert in burnout. To understand burnout and make it easy for people to identify, I created a framework called the Pyramid of UN-potential. There are five levels of UN-potential and a foundational starting point where the seeds of burnout take root.

Our deepest limiting beliefs typically come from our childhood, whether from our parents, extended family, teachers, or friends. They get retriggered in our adult life, creating disharmony and dysfunction. These beliefs are so deep within us that we often don't even know they exist. When we peel the layers back, the most common limiting beliefs sound like these: "I'm not good enough," "I'm not lovable," "I don't matter," "I don't belong," "There's something wrong with me," and biggest of all, "I'm not worthy." They lurk in the background of our life and subconsciously control our decisions as well as our reactions.

These core limiting beliefs stem from feelings of not being accepted for who we are. This can leave us feeling unworthy of love, unaccepting of our gifts, and undeserving of success, happiness, and kindness. This keeps our potential from being unleashed.

These limited beliefs get agitated by our jobs and our home-lives and plant the seeds of burnout, which I call the UNs.

Ultimately, the UNs grow like weeds in our garden of self-realization, keeping us stuck in our UN-potential. To help you distinguish the weeds from the flowers, here are the most common UNs and how they make us feel:

- Unseen = invisible and rejected
- Unheard = our voice doesn't matter
- Unwanted = disposable and not enough
- Unloved = something is wrong with us
- Unimportant = not valuable

The Pyramid of UN-potential

The UNs disconnect us from our radiance and the truth of who we are. All human beings — at our core — need to feel seen, heard, and acknowledged. We need to feel like we matter. When the UNs get kicked up, they cause a ruckus, which leads to the Unders — the first level in the Pyramid of UN-potential. Here are all five levels of the pyramid:

> Level 1: The Unders — feelings of being undervalued, underappreciated, underrecognized, underestimated, and underpaid
> Level 2: The Overs — a state of overworking, overstressing, overthinking, overwhelming, and overextending
> Level 3: Questioning Belonging — uncertainty about belonging, questioning whether to stay or leave
> Level 4: Disharmony in the Bodies — impacts to mental, emotional, physical, spiritual, and financial well-being
> Level 5: Devastation of the D's — divorce, depression, disease, debt, and even death

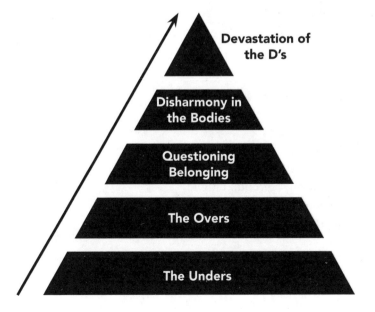

Level 1: The Unders

Once you recognize one of the five levels of UN-potential, you can take action long before the impact becomes severe. At level one, the Unders are triggered when we feel unwanted, unseen, or unheard. Typically, one or more of the Unders will surface as frustrated feelings. Here are the five most common Unders and their associated negative impacts:

- Undervalued = lowered self-esteem
- Underappreciated = resentment and anger
- Underrecognized = disengaged and aloof
- Underestimated = discouraged and frustrated
- Underpaid = compromised self-worth

Real fast, check in with yourself: Are you feeling any of the Unders? If so, which ones? Write them down. You'll explore this further in this chapter's exercise.

Level 2: The Overs

Level two in the Pyramid of UN-potential is the Overs. When we feel any of the Unders — for example, feeling undervalued — it's natural to overcompensate to keep other people from seeing what we feel. We tend to hide feeling unlovable, undeserving, unworthy, or whatever the core limiting belief is. Here are the most common forms of the Overs:

- Overworking = exhaustion
- Overstressing = constantly on edge
- Overthinking = mental fatigue
- Overwhelming = anxiety
- Overextending = never enough time

This list is just a start; there are many more Overs. If you are overdoing anything, that's an Over. The easiest way to catch yourself from going into severe burnout is to pay attention to the Overs. If you are Overing, it is because something feels Undered. You can rest assured that if an UN needs your attention and goes unaddressed, it will disconnect you from your radiance. To protect our potential, we must learn how to understand, identify, and prevent our fire from burning out. When you find yourself Overing this is a clue that burnout is taking root.

Level 3: Questioning Belonging

Level three of the Pyramid of UN-potential is Questioning Belonging. This is when we start questioning ourselves. Perhaps we're stretching ourselves thin and feeling like we're not quite fitting in, and suddenly, we're pondering: *Should I stay, or should I go? Do I even belong here?* This is when inner conflicts can begin to intensify.

When you're stuck in this zone, it's a recipe for inner chaos. You're all tangled up in accepting the unacceptable and putting up with things that you shouldn't. In this level of UN-potential, our radiance starts losing its spark, and Netflix marathons become our comfort zone.

Recognizing these five common traits of Questioning Belonging will help prevent you from getting stuck in this space for too long:

- Hopelessness = bypassing the issue, no ownership
- Tolerating = giving up our personal power
- Confusion = cloudy thinking and poor decisions
- Stuck = lost connection with possibility
- Feeling outcast = feeling alone

Level 4: Disharmony in the Bodies

When our sense of belonging is constantly questioned, our UN-potential escalates to level four, Disharmony in the Bodies.

The reason the bodies are plural is because we have five bodies that get impacted by burnout: mental, emotional, physical, spiritual, and financial.

This disharmony starts causing a ruckus in one if not all of the bodies. Our mental game takes a hit, anxiety makes a surprise guest appearance, our shoulders get tense, hope takes a nosedive, and hey, maybe that shopping spree feels like a quick fix (Amazon cart alert!). This is just a sneak peek into how our bodies react when we're stuck in that level of UN-potential.

Here's a quick glance at the disharmony in those five bodies and what some side effects might look like:

- Mental = brain fog, irritability, insomnia
- Emotional = depression, withdrawal, anxiety
- Physical = tension, disease, pain
- Spiritual = disconnection, hopelessness, severe loneliness
- Financial = debt, paycheck-to-paycheck living, bankruptcy

Level 5: Devastation of the D's

In level five, when we brush off those signs our mind, body, and soul are waving at us, things start feeling seriously off. This isn't just discomfort; it's a full-blown dis-ease. I'm talking about the potential for heart disease, autoimmune troubles, and even cancer.

Our relationships with family and friends might start getting disconnected, maybe even leading to the big D — divorce. Those shopping sprees? Suddenly, we're swimming in dangerous amounts of debt. Drinking and drugs — both prescribed and recreational — can be used as Band-Aids to cover the pain our soul is feeling. At its worst, level five can even mean the end — like a sudden, unexpected heart attack. This level isn't playing around. It's a wake-up call to stop ignoring those signals our whole being is sending our way.

Here are the top five devastating D's and their impacts:

- Divorce = feelings of failure
- Debt = overwhelming pressure
- Depression = unable to feel joy
- Disease = loss of freedom
- Death = loss of life

Here's the thing about burnout: It is not permanent, though if not addressed, it can lead to permanent losses. The good news is we can break up with it. We are born worthy of having optimized health, wealth, and happiness. We deserve to have our super big dreamy goals fulfilled. We are enough. It's safe to be ourselves. Turn up your extra; you were not born to play small.

As you will learn as you practice the POWER Method, when you start to slip back into old habits, you have the ability to hit the pause button so that the old track doesn't play again. You can choose to skip to the next song and protect your precious potential.

Grab Your Gemstone: According to one survey, burnout is at a staggering 69 percent, with another 29 percent of working professionals showing signs of it. Reconnecting with your passions and protecting your potential helps to prevent the signs and symptoms of burnout. The framework of the Pyramid of UN-potential can help you recognize and address the underlying causes that leave you feeling disconnected from life. It offers practical strategies to break free from the grip of burnout and pursue a fulfilling, radiant life aligned with your dreams and values.

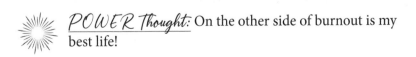

POWER Thought: On the other side of burnout is my best life!

POWER Up Your Practice 1:
Getting Over Burnout

The very best way to prevent burnout is to stop before it hits level three. In level one, the Unders, and level two, the Overs, you are still on the verge of burnout. Once you get to level three, Questioning Belonging, you are in active burnout. My suggestion is always to work backward from the Overs to the UNs to figure out what's going on.

This exercise is a surefire way to stop burnout in its tracks. Ask these questions to help you protect your potential and prevent burnout:

- What are my current Overs?
  Example: I am overworked and overwhelmed.
- What Unders am I feeling?
  Example: I am feeling undervalued and underpaid at work.
- Why do I feel the Unders?
  Example: I feel that my boss doesn't listen to me. I feel unheard.
- When I feel the UNs, what am I feeling?
  Example: When I feel unheard, it makes me feel not good enough.

Using these questions, you can increase your self-awareness of what is making you feel not good enough, and then you can take action to get that need met. Whether you give yourself some restful self-love or you take action to refresh your resumé, you are no longer ignoring that voice inside that is starving for attention. Simple acts can help you refrain from going further into your UN-potential.

Remember, you can download all this book's exercises in the complimentary Return to Radiance Personal Transformation Guide at Resources.ReturnToRadianceBook.com.

CHAPTER TWO

The BS That Holds You Back

I *don't have enough time. I can't do that. I don't have a choice.* These are among the most common responses I hear when I am working with teams to facilitate change. These limited beliefs keep us stuck in our UN-potential and can cause serious health, wealth, and relationship issues when unaddressed.

There is a cost to believing that a force outside us is more powerful than the force inside. The truth is you are not limited by the BS that holds you back. You are part of Infinite Intelligence, and Infinite Intelligence is part of you. There is part of you that is resourceful, resilient, and rebellious enough — in a good way — to find solutions and to break free from perceived limitations.

The Issues Got Stuck in My Tissues

As we sat in the conference room of her office, Kate, my functional medicine practitioner, delivered some life-altering news. "Becca, you have breast implant illness," she said. In disbelief, I quickly scanned the room for any signs of a prank, but it was just the two of us. As Kate continued to explain the situation, my heart raced and my palms grew sweaty. I started to feel sick to my stomach.

"After reviewing your blood work results, symptoms, and chief complaints, I'm positive that it's being caused by your breast implants. You are also showing signs of active autoimmune disease," she said.

My mind raced as I struggled to grasp the reality of my

situation. I'd never heard of breast implant illness before, and yet here I was, living with it. Kate continued, "The high levels of stress from your last job and the traumatic loss of both your parents wreaked havoc on your body." Her words triggered a flood of thoughts, and I suddenly realized that she might be right.

Memories of my hair falling out, fatigue that made my bones ache, and brain fog so thick that it felt like I was living in a cloud all came flooding back. Kate said, "Becca, your reserves are low. Your body is fighting itself, and we need to take action or things are going to get a lot worse."

I struggled to find the words to respond, feeling overwhelmed by the news. However, I was grateful that someone had finally heard my cries for help after three long years of searching for answers. Kate was unlike all the other doctors who had dismissed my concerns, telling me that it was all in my head. She offered me a different path — one of self-reliance, self-advocacy, and self-love.

Kate went on to say, "Once we address the core medical issues, we will need to address your body and beliefs that got you this sick. You see, our issues can get stuck in the tissues of our body. Our goal here is to reconnect you to your radiance." As I closed my eyes, I chuckled to myself, realizing that the name of Kate's practice was Radiant Health. I appreciated the excellent branding reinforcement, but more importantly, I knew that there was truth in what she was saying. Kate didn't know it, but the word *radiance* had a deep spiritual meaning for me due to its connection to Kundalini yoga, where radiance is the highest expression of our soul in the human experience.

Despite the challenges ahead, I felt empowered by the potential of what was possible. I just needed to move past the BS that got me into this situation in the first place. I was ready to return to my radiance and walk away from this with optimized health. So I opened my eyes, smiled at Kate, and said, "What's next?"

Traumas, Dramas, and the Body

Did you know that a whopping 80 percent of the residue from our traumas and dramas is stored in our bodies? It's not all in our mind; it's in our very flesh and bones. Our traumas, our dramas, they don't just evaporate into thin air. They take up residence in our bodies.

They in essence become part of the wiring within our body until we make a conscious effort to include our body in our healing process and use this knowledge to further protect our potential. It was during my training and my transformation with Kundalini yoga that this truth became crystal clear — as I purposefully used yoga poses, breathwork, and meditations to intentionally release my traumas and dramas from my body.

It wasn't just me. Everyone in the training program was experiencing massive growth and transformation. We were breaking patterns, letting go of decade-old emotions, and releasing pain that had been stuck in our bodies for what felt like a lifetime. We often had tears running down our faces as we encountered a major release, indicating that something had shifted and was ready to be let go of.

I also learned that sometimes the body is months — if not years — behind in manifesting all the dis-ease we experience on the inside as disease on the outside. This made sense because when Kate told me that I had autoimmune disease and breast implant illness, I wasn't shocked. I knew that I had been through so much devastation. My body was just catching up to the mental, emotional, and spiritual disarray I had experienced in the years before the diagnosis.

This topic fascinated me. Before getting introduced to this concept that our body needs to be part of the healing process to fully rise back into our potential, I thought traditional talk therapy and meditation were the two best ways to do this. Wanting to understand this even more, I dove headfirst into getting certified in trauma awareness and limited beliefs so that I could help myself and others truly get unstuck from UN-potential and become everything we are meant to be.

During my training, the book *The Body Keeps the Score* by Bessel van der Kolk was required reading for every single one of us, and it was mind-altering for me. Bessel's research has shown that Kundalini yoga, my cosmic weapon of choice, is one of the most scientifically proven ways to kick those traumas and dramas to the curb and return us to our radiance. This is why I am such a big advocate of it because I have seen it transform myself, my teaching peers, and my students.

Your Survival Styles

To protect your potential, you need to understand how you get stuck in your UN-potential. As I say, burnout can silently and accidentally become a severe problem when it goes unaddressed, and 80 percent of our trauma gets stuck in our body. When trauma is trapped in our head and in our body, it puts us in a survival state.

Our nervous system is a master at keeping us safe and sound. From the moment we take our first breath until around age seven, we're learning how to navigate this crazy world and get our needs met. For example, if we talk too much as a kid and it pisses off our mom, we quickly learn to keep our mouth shut, all in the pursuit of that sweet, sweet love and acceptance every little kid needs from their mom. These are our survival instincts in action.

Our nervous systems take all that programming we soak up like sponges and treats it like gospel. It becomes our subconscious default, running the show behind the scenes, and this becomes part of the BS that holds us back. But here's where the plot thickens. Fast-forward to adulthood: When someone raises their voice, triggers get pulled, and that childhood conditioning comes rushing back like a bat out of hell. The yelling triggers the "yelling is bad" reaction, and before we know it, we're either ready to throw down or throw up.

Let's take a look at four ways our nervous system gets stuck in a survival state and how it tries to protect us:

- Fight: meet the threat with aggression
- Flight: run away from the threat
- Freeze: become unable to move or act against the threat
- Fawn: try to appease the threat to avoid more conflict

Take a moment and consider which reaction resonates with you the most. Which of these is your go-to survival style?

Before I started my own healing journey, I was a fawner and a fighter. Imagine this feisty redhead, face turning redder than a ripe tomato, losing her cool, saying things she didn't mean, and damaging relationships left and right. Something had to change. But here's the thing, we're not here to banish our survival states. They have a positive side. They act as our trusty survival guides, keeping us from certain demise. What we want, what we need, is awareness of our styles so that we recognize them when they arise — *Oh wait, I'm fawning.*

Then with self-awareness helping us out, we can hit the pause button before we react. We can ask ourselves a question like, "Am I going to let my inner seven-year-old call the shots, or am I going to let the adult me handle this?"

I won't lie to you. Developing this self-awareness is a challenge at first, but trust me, it gets easier with time. These reactions were originally an inheritance from our ancestors, who had to escape packs of wolves. That's not us today, not at all. But we still unconsciously react to childhood threats as if we're being hunted down by a wild pack of snarling beasts. Can you believe it? Our outdated programming, wreaking havoc on our adult lives. Insane, isn't it?

Good news: The problem isn't you. The problem lies in that outdated programming from your childhood. Your nervous system is screaming for a software upgrade, and I've got your back. Throughout this journey, you'll be armed with juicy how-tos and life-changing tips to achieve that system upgrade your life is craving.

You Need to Calm Down

To quote the fabulous Taylor Swift, "You need to calm down." To help come out of survival mode, we need some help rewiring and retraining our nervous system to calm down. We need practical tools to help regulate it. The superhighway of the nervous system is the polyvagal nerve. In his book *The Polyvagal Theory*, Stephen W. Porges discusses in detail how this autonomic nervous system is responsible for our feelings of safety and how it is influenced by our central nervous system.

The vagus nerve is the longest cranial nerve in the body and plays a crucial role in regulating various bodily glands and functions. If we know how to regulate our polyvagal nerve, we can control our life — or at least how we react to it. When we can intentionally stimulate the vagus nerve, we will remain calm under stress, and we will be able to recognize that we aren't in life-threatening danger. It also prevents us from losing our cool and being embarrassed about it later!

If you are ready to move past the BS that has been holding you back, then mindful interactions with your vagus nerve will help you break free from the barriers of your youth and allow you to reconnect with your inner truth — that part of you that is radiant, all-knowing, and timeless.

The wonderful news is that several techniques are proven to calm the polyvagal nerve and help us stay out of survival mode. Here are the most common practices for self-regulation:

- Breathwork
- Yoga

- Singing, chanting, humming
- Cold water exposure
- Laughter
- Meditation

I describe several in this book, and as you become more aware of when your BS starts to hold you back, you can use any of them to help you get unstuck and back to shining as the beautiful light that you are.

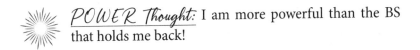 *Grab Your Gemstone:* You can overcome common limiting beliefs and recognize your internal power to foster personal growth. Unresolved traumas affect physical health and introduce survival styles that can keep you in a stress response. Techniques like yoga and breathwork can help you regulate your nervous system and reconnect with your inner radiance and truth.

POWER Thought: I am more powerful than the BS that holds me back!

POWER Up Your Practice 2: Square Breathing

When it comes to moving past the BS that holds you back, your breath is one of your most powerful assets. Conscious breathing can help you transition out of survival mode and moments of overwhelm and help your nervous system recalibrate to thrive. This breathing technique is simple yet extremely effective. Add it to the collection of tips, tools, and techniques you discover in this book.

Square breathing works so well that it is used by US Navy SEALs, high-stress professionals like first responders, and people who suffer from PTSD. It's also a go-to for us yogis. Also known as box breathing, square breathing is a controlled four-part breath that helps regulate the nervous system by reducing anxiety, increasing alertness, and allowing your body to release toxins (and BS) more readily.

Square breathing is super simple and easy to learn, and you can use this any time and as often as needed. This is a trick to keep in your back pocket.

Here's how to do it:

- To start, relax by breathing in and breathing out deeply a few times.
- Close your eyes, roll your shoulders back, release any tension in your face, and place your hands in your lap or another comfortable position.
- When you are ready, follow this four-part sequence:

    Inhale for a count of four.
    Hold the breath for a count of four.
    Exhale for a count of four.
    Hold for a count of four.

    Repeat this for a minimum of four sets, but you can continue as many times as you want.

CHAPTER THREE

Power Up Your Choices

*H*ave you ever said yes to something when you totally meant no? This is so common that we barely — if at all — stop to consider ourselves and our needs. Saying yes too fast is one of the ways that we override what our innate inner wisdom is trying to tell us. As you start to protect your potential, learning to power up your choices is a critical part of the process.

Your choices, whether you know it or not, are responsible for whether your life thrives or not. This chapter is about learning how choice can serve you, how saying yes to yourself is not selfish, and how prioritizing your well-being is a must.

The Day After the Bathroom Floor

As I share, I stayed stuck in my UN-potential for three years, and not nurturing my radiance led to extreme burnout and severe health issues. How did I get there? I was an expert at saying yes. I said yes to my bosses, yes to my team, yes to my husband, and yes to my kids. Yet during that time, I can't remember saying yes to myself.

When I finally hit my emotional rock bottom, it happened on the tail of this three-year run of saying yes to everything but myself. After my fourth bad day in a row, I was running on empty as I parked my car in the driveway. It took me a moment to collect myself because I knew as soon as I walked through the door, I needed to be a mom and wife. Taking a deep breath and doing the best I could to put on a happy face, I shut off the car, put my purse on my right shoulder, and walked into the house.

The kids were waiting for me as soon as I walked in. I never even saw their wide eyes and big smiles. All I heard was Mom this and Mom that — and I lost my temper. I yelled at them, "Can I put my freaking purse down? Mom needs five minutes!" As soon as the response left my lips, I immediately felt shame and guilt because I could see how much it hurt them.

Later that night after the kids went to bed, I was washing my face and could barely recognize the person staring back at me in the mirror. It was me, but it wasn't me. That spark inside was gone. I was short-fused, miserable, and running on empty. I began to cry. The next thing I knew, I had officially lost the last little bit of energy I had and ended up falling to the bathroom floor crying.

Now, if I'm being real, this was one of the most powerless moments I have ever felt in my life. In complete desperation, I prayed to the Universe for help. I remember saying, "I can't do tomorrow the same way I'm doing today — and I only know how to do tomorrow the same way I'm doing today. I need help." I exchanged a few more words and then something incredible happened. I received what I call my instant miracle. A voice seemed to whisper to me, *Becca, you are the CEO of your life.*

This thought was so powerful that it sent a wave of empowerment through my exhausted body. I remember thinking, *Well, if I am the CEO of my life, then I have a lot more power in this situation than I thought. Becca, get your butt up!* I rose off the bathroom floor a different woman than the one who went down. It was one of the most spiritual moments I can recall. I felt like I had become the phoenix herself — rising from her own ashes, renewed and transformed.

I didn't have the luxury of going on a backpacking sabbatical to find myself and rebuild my life. I had to go to work the next day — to the same place that had just contributed to my bathroom-floor moment. I knew I would have to do something different, but what that was I had no idea.

The next day at work it became glaringly clear. Something had shifted within me. I felt a need to protect my well-being fiercely. During a leadership meeting, I was asked to lead another project, something that I would previously have said yes to without even thinking. Instead, the word *no* flew out of my mouth. Somewhat shocked and scrambling for what to say next so I didn't get fired, I followed it up by saying, "My plate is really full right now and it might be better if a junior leader takes it. This might be a good opportunity for them to learn."

I had just said yes to preserving my energy and not overextending myself — and it felt scary as heck. My heart was pounding waiting for a dramatic reply. The most senior leader in the room replied, "That's a great idea, we'll ask Melanie." Without hesitation, we proceeded to the next agenda topic.

What I learned from this experience is that part of nurturing our radiance is saying yes more often to ourselves and no more often to other people and projects. Not saying yes to myself and my own well-being played a significant role that led to one of my most powerless moments. I also learned that powering up my choices and learning to say no to things that were going to drain me was just as essential as putting on my makeup for the day.

Here's a profound takeaway from that experience: We hold the power to either empower or disempower ourselves by the choices we make.

It's Not Selfish, It's Self-First

According to a 2023 survey published by the American Psychological Association (APA), 92 percent of workers said it was very (57 percent) or somewhat (35 percent) important to them to work for an organization that values their emotional and psychological well-being. The article said this shows how both employees and employers are much more conscious about health and well-being in the aftermath of the Covid pandemic.

Despite the increased awareness, the APA said workplace burnout is still estimated to be around 77 percent, which mirrors the survey my company conducted that found that 69 percent of working professionals were actively burned out. The article said survey responders specified the following complaints:

- Emotional exhaustion (31 percent)
- Lack of motivation to do their best (26 percent)
- A desire to keep to themselves (25 percent)
- A desire to quit (23 percent)
- Lower productivity (20 percent)
- Irritability or anger with coworkers and customers (19 percent)
- Feeling ineffective (18 percent)

The APA article cited the US Surgeon General's "Framework for Workplace Mental Health and Well-Being," which names five areas that are essential to prevent burnout and health issues:

- Protection from harm (including security and safety)
- Connection and community (including social support and belonging)
- Work-life harmony (including autonomy and flexibility)
- Mattering at work (including dignity and meaning)
- Opportunity for growth (including learning and accomplishment)

If you are among the 69 percent of workers who are feeling the signs and symptoms of burnout, heed the Surgeon General's advice and protect your potential.

Ever heard the phrase "You can't drink from an empty cup"? This means we can't truly shine in our brilliance or show up for others or ourselves when we have no energy to give. On the other hand, when we are full of energy, health, and well-being, we can show up for ourselves and others from the overflow of our cup, rather than draining the last few drops. The next time you are running on empty, remember this: Choosing to prioritize your well-being isn't selfish, it's self-first.

Here is a question for you, fierce one: What one choice can you make today that is self-first?

Choice Has Two Paths

When I was finally ready to take the reins as the CEO of my life and make self-first decisions, I found myself reading many books on personal growth and spirituality. One in particular, *The Seat of the Soul* by Gary Zukav, motivated me to consider two things very consciously — my intentions and my choices. Here is an excerpt, which I hope inspires you to consider your soul, your human self, and your choices:

> When the energy of the soul is recognized, acknowledged, and valued, it begins to infuse the life of the personality. When the personality comes to fully serve the energy of its soul, that is authentic empowerment. This is the goal of the evolutionary process in which we are involved and the reason for our being. Every experience that you have and will have upon the Earth encourages alignment of your personality with your soul. Every circumstance and situation gives you the opportunity to choose this path, to allow your soul to shine through you, to bring into the physical world through you its unending and unfathomable reverence for and love of Life.

There are quite a few important takeaways from this paragraph when it comes to choosing your path. This starts with acknowledging that we are more than just our personality, we are a soul — a limitless and timeless form. Part of us is undefined by the limitations of being human. If you recognize that your soul might not be getting tended to, allow yourself to reincorporate that super-important element back into your life.

Next, this line is a game changer: "Every circumstance and situation gives you the opportunity to choose this path, to allow your soul to shine through you." In every moment, we can make choices that empower us rather than disempower us. The truth is choice only has two paths — one path serves, empowers, and helps, and the other path sabotages, disempowers, and hurts. When you make a choice that does not allow your soul to shine through you, you will feel the energy zap almost immediately. Start paying attention to your energy. Ask yourself: Does this decision make me feel good or does it make me feel bad? Start to honor how you feel when you make your choices.

Then there's this line: "When the personality comes to fully serve the energy of its soul, that is authentic empowerment." When our human self decides to serve the gifts of the soul — our strengths, gifts, talents, and uniqueness — then our life takes an empowering twist into authentic alignment with our radiance. We begin to attract people, situations, and opportunities that serve us. We no longer spend countless hours serving other people and organizations that don't fill our cup in return. When life starts happening for you in this zone of authentic alignment, you will find new levels of success, creativity, fulfillment, and liberation emerge. Life becomes more than empowering; it becomes extremely satisfying!

The next time you need to make a decision, remember that choice has two paths.

- One path disempowers you and cuts you off from the limitless potential of your soul, leaving you feeling depleted and disconnected.
- The other path empowers you and your soul to unite and embrace possibility as well as unleash your potential.

Consider this your invitation to power up your choices and protect your precious potential!

Grab Your Gemstone: Empowered choices help protect your potential and well-being. Recognizing the role your choices play in shaping the quality of your life is in your power and control. Align your choices with your soul's desires for authentic joy and fulfillment.

POWER Thought: My choices serve, help, and empower me!

POWER Up Your Practice 3: Seven-Day Self-First 50/50 Challenge

From learning how to power up your choices to having a self-first mindset — these are key ingredients to truly protect your potential. For this exercise, for one full week, pay close attention to your choices and whether or not they are serving you or sabotaging you. Most of the time, when we don't consider ourselves when making decisions, we tend to hurt ourselves, even if it's only a little bit.

In addition, I encourage you to make sure that at least half of your decisions over the week are self-first. That is the 50/50 challenge: Half the time consider yourself first, and half the time make choices as you usually would.

This challenge will help you consider yourself and your well-being before making a choice. The more you practice, the more your choices will empower you.

Changing habits takes time and effort. I recommend keeping a journal or using your notes app on your phone to track this experiment. It's helpful to capture the choices you make, how they make you feel, and what happens as a result. This will help you further embrace the practice.

Want more growth? Try considering yourself first in most of your decisions. As you dive into this, watch closely as transformation unfolds. Your self-worth and your confidence will get a turbo boost. As a bonus, you'll find that you can serve others with more of an open heart, less resentment, and oodles more fulfillment.

CHAPTER FOUR

Boundaries Are Your Best Friend

As you move away from burnout and the BS that holds you back, you begin to power up your choices, and the more you say yes to yourself, the more your stress and anxiety lessen. You begin to feel more like yourself. Practicing this prepares you for your next power move — making boundaries your best friend.

The concepts of powering up our choices and setting boundaries are in the same family, so to speak, but they are different. I like to think of powering up our choices as a way of honoring ourselves and making sure our decisions are in harmony with our truth. Making boundaries our best friend is a way of respecting ourselves, our time, and our energy as well as no longer tolerating or accepting the things that dim our light.

Boundaries play a critical role in protecting your potential. One of the coolest benefits of boundary making is that your self-worth and self-confidence skyrocket. With increased self-esteem, you start to step out of your UN-potential and step into your truest potential.

No More Bargaining

"I just put in my two-week notice, Becca!" Gina exclaimed. This was like music to my ears. My former coworker and now friend was taking a huge stand for herself. I was ecstatic and couldn't have been more proud. "Tell me more," I said.

Gina went on to explain how a lunch conversation we had a few weeks earlier had led to big changes in her life. She was working in a toxic work environment where she was undervalued and underappreciated. She had begun bargaining with herself: *If I can just make it to the one-year mark, then I can look for a new role.* This made absolutely no sense to me because Gina was a senior salesperson with a phenomenal reputation in our tech sales community for customer advocacy and high performance.

Gina was six months into her new role and knew it was not a fit, but she was concerned about how a short stay at the company would look on her resumé. I challenged Gina by asking her what was going to change between now and that one-year mark. Too often, we arrive at a conclusion of what to do without actually considering alternative scenarios and comparing consequences. For Gina, if she stayed for a year or left now, which would suffer more long-term damage: her well-being or her resumé?

Gina is fierce and typically not one to play small. When she realized she was tolerating and accepting things she shouldn't, she said, "It's time to stop bargaining." She knew nothing was going to change at the job. To improve her situation, she needed to leave this job for a better one.

Within a few weeks, a new job found her; she didn't even have to go looking for it.

This new company had a people-centric culture, an awesome product, was willing to give her a great territory, and offered a higher overall compensation package. It was so clear that this job was made for Gina that she did not hesitate to say yes.

What I want you to know is this: *The Universe shows up for you when you show up for yourself.* When you protect your energy by using boundaries, it gives space for your soul to serve your personality. Infinite Intelligence creates moments of synchronicity that align in your favor, just like Gina experienced.

The Role of Shame and Guilt

Shame. It's that sneaky little saboteur that plays a starring role in our unhappiness and unfulfillment — and it doesn't play fair. Shame has this uncanny ability to nibble away at our self-worth and chisel away at self-esteem.

In Gina's case, she had only been at the toxic job a little over six months, and she felt shame that a short-lived tenure might reflect negatively upon her.

Shame's sister, guilt, also emerges when our people-pleasing tendencies are high. This happens because, in our belief system, we are disposed to serve others before ourselves. Guilt often whispers that it's not good to hurt someone else's feelings — but it's OK to hurt our own. And that's just not true!

Most people avoid boundaries because of how they might make them appear — selfish, inconsiderate, foolish, or mean. They fear how others may perceive them and that they could be exposed as not good enough, not worthy, or weak. They want to look so good in the eyes of others that they will purposely sacrifice their wants and needs. In my experience of working with burned-out leaders and high performers, I have learned that compromise often leads to collapse.

This is why powering up your choices isn't selfish. Because if you aren't willing to put yourself first, then you will find it very hard to set boundaries. When you have no boundaries, you leave yourself vulnerable to getting stuck in your UN-potential. It's important — especially when you are called to serve and make a big impact — to show up and serve in your best health and energy.

We do that by first allowing ourselves to have self-first consideration, and then we use boundaries as a way to honor our energy and well-being. Then we can change the role shame and guilt play in our life. Shame and guilt are indicators that we are considering others — which in and of itself is not a bad thing! That's a sign that we are a kind and compassionate person. When you feel shame and guilt emerge, and you find yourself bargaining with yourself, pause and recognize them as warning signs.

Instead of thinking about how others might feel or how others might perceive you, consider what the cost of compromising your own well-being might be. Will it zap all your energy? Will it take your presence away from your loved ones and the things that matter most to you? Will it cause unnecessary stress and anxiety?

After you answer those self-reflective questions, offer yourself that same kindness, consideration, and compassion you so freely offer others. Let shame and guilt be your warning sirens. Think of them as an internal trigger that a boundary may be needed to protect you from UN-potential.

Make Boundaries Your Best Friend

Why make boundaries your best friend? Because feeling exhausted sprinkled with bouts of shame and guilt sucks. Plus, just like a best friend, boundaries have your back! They help protect you from making bad choices, prevent you from getting taken advantage of, help you do more of the things you love to do, and keep you shooting for the stars. And you don't need a ton of them, you just need one really good one.

If you were taught that boundaries are to be set between you and someone else, you are not alone. The truth is they aren't. We never have control over another person's actions even if we think we do — and that's why boundaries don't seem to work. The only person we have control over is ourselves.

Only you know if your well-being is being compromised, if you are tolerating something you shouldn't, or if you have too much on your plate. If you let someone else dictate what you are doing, in essence, you're giving them the reins to your life. Take control back by allowing your new boundary BFF to help you say yes and no to things in a way that supports your health, time, and energy.

The only boundary that ever sticks is the one between you and yourself. I often need to remind high performers of this. No one else knows our workload as well as we do — and saying yes to too many things is 100 percent going to affect our performance. To keep performance high, we need to protect our potential by learning what we can and can't take on.

Best friends have a way of making our life better and more enjoyable, and so can using this boundary philosophy. In business, I have seen the art of saying no transform people from mediocre leaders to extraordinary ones. There's a practice I like to call "Pass On It, Pass It On" (see next page). Just because you can do something doesn't mean you should. Acknowledging this, especially at work, keeps you aligned with your potential and helps others develop theirs.

When you make boundaries your best friend, you put an end to constant chaos and reduce feelings of shame and guilt. Boundaries shout an epic battle cry against overcommitment so you can live a life where you reign supreme. You also start to recognize that when someone is OK with overwhelming you, that isn't very nice, and it makes it a heck of a lot easier to advocate for yourself.

So be willing to let boundaries become your best friend and embrace the limitless possibilities that come with protecting your potential.

Grab Your Gemstone: Your choices and ability to make boundaries your best friend help you overcome burnout and lead a fulfilling life. By honoring yourself through empowered decision-making and setting boundaries that respect your time and energy, you reduce stress and anxiety while boosting your self-worth and confidence. Ultimately, embracing boundaries as allies empowers you to live authentically, advocate for yourself, and pursue your fullest potential without compromising your health and happiness.

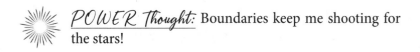 *POWER Thought:* Boundaries keep me shooting for the stars!

POWER Up Your Practice 4:
Pass On It, Pass It On

This exercise builds off the one in chapter 3, "Seven-Day Self-First 50/50 Challenge" (page 35), and it helps you practice passing on opportunities or requests when they are not a fit. This includes practicing how to pass that opportunity or request to someone else in a nonburdensome way that helps others learn and grow. This is a great way to create a win-win out of a situation that otherwise would have added more stress and anxiety on your plate.

Here's the practice "Pass On It, Pass It On":

- Reflect on your priorities: Take a moment to reflect on your current commitments, goals, and priorities. Consider what opportunities align with these priorities and which ones may not be the best fit for you at this time.

- Identify opportunities to pass on: Think about any upcoming opportunities or requests for help that you may encounter in your personal or professional life. These could be tasks, projects, invitations, or favors that you feel may not align with your goals or strengths.

- Practice saying no: Practice saying no to these opportunities respectfully and assertively. Use phrases like these:

    "Thank you for thinking of me, but I don't think this opportunity aligns with my current priorities."

    "I appreciate the offer, but I believe someone else may be better suited for this task."

    "While I'm unable to take on this project myself, I'd be happy to help you find someone else who may be interested and available."

- Offer assistance in finding a replacement: Instead of simply declining the opportunity, offer to help find someone else who may be a better fit. This could involve suggesting specific individuals or offering to assist in the search process.

- Reflect on your experience: After practicing saying no and offering assistance, take some time to reflect on the experience. Notice any emotions that arise and how asserting your boundaries and offering help to others made you feel.

- Repeat and reinforce: Continue to practice saying no and offering assistance whenever you encounter opportunities that are not a good fit for you. Over time, this will become easier, and you'll become more comfortable advocating for yourself while also supporting others in their growth and development.

This exercise will help you make boundaries your best friend as well as practice the art of saying no to protect your space, energy, and time. It fosters a sense of empowerment and collaboration while ensuring that you prioritize your own well-being and alignment with your goals.

CHAPTER FIVE

Permission to Have
Super Big Dreamy Goals

According to research at Scranton University, only 8 percent of people actually hit their goals. Then again, they found that only 17 percent of people take the time to think about their goals enough to set them. This means almost half of the people who set goals experience them come to fruition. That is pretty promising! I'd like to think if the other half who set goals had additional support and guidance, that percentage would increase.

This chapter is about giving yourself permission to not only dream but to have super big dreamy goals that motivate you to take action. Statistically speaking, 92 percent of people need to give their dreams, desires, and goals more attention. If that applies to you, ask yourself: When did you stop setting and chasing your goals? At what point did your dreams start to feel too big, too hard, or too crazy?

Consider this your permission slip to start chasing your goals and dreams again. Pursuing your goals is what unleashes your potential. It's when life begins to unfold in magical and unexpected ways.

The Care Bear Goes There

"The Care Bear goes there. The Pound Puppy goes here. Mr. Teddy Bear can go right here, and my all-time favorite, Rainbow Brite, will get her front-row spot, as always," I said, as I proudly set up my stuffed animals. In my eight-year-old imagination, I was turning my bedroom into a theater. I was delivering life-changing talks with the magic of my words — and my stuffed animal audience loved every ounce of it.

It wasn't just about fluffy friends and pretend shows. After watching my dad perform on stage in front of real people, something deep inside me stirred. I, too, saw myself on stage. But instead of epic guitar solos, I'd be talking — sharing my own written stories.

That dream unleashed a torrent of creativity. Poems, short stories, song lyrics, you name it. I'd jot them down in journals and perform them passionately to my stuffed animal fan club. Each time I delivered a talk to them, my confidence grew. Yet as the years rolled by, my solo bedroom performances got swapped out for hanging out with friends and trying to fit in. Writing wasn't considered cool. Speaking in public was considered dorky — and before I knew it, I had all but abandoned this thing I'd loved since I was a kid.

What I didn't realize was that in those early days, my radiance flowed through me just like it did with my dad. I was a channel for the Universe's creativity, and it was a thrilling, natural high. But somewhere along the way, I hit pause. My twenties were consumed by college, starting a family, and my career — and my love for writing and speaking got deprioritized.

That nagging feeling persisted though. The sense that I was destined for more, that my gifts and talents were itching to express themselves — and I bet you've felt that, too.

After years of leading, teaching, and training working professionals, I've witnessed a familiar pattern. Adults stop dreaming. They settle for the ordinary, stifle their inner magic, and deep down, they're restless and unsatisfied.

Your goals and dreams ignite your soul and allow you to

express the truth of who you are. If you had to pick one, what goal or dream would you prioritize or, if necessary, invite back into your life?

Super Big Dreamy Goals

Big goals can be terrifying and thrilling depending on your perspective — and they should be! Super big dreamy goals are intoxicating, and they invite us to pursue them. Simultaneously, they leave us questioning how to pursue them because of their size. Goals and dreams are the very thing our radiance is here to express itself through. They give our life deeper meaning and a medium to embrace our gifts, talents, and strengths. Their lofty nature provides a sense of purpose and direction.

The Apollo moon landing, the iPhone, and Disney World are just a few examples of radical, crazy, and once far-fetched ideas that changed the world and opened new possibilities for others. Super big dreamy goals ignite our soul and connect us to Infinite Intelligence. There's a sense that they are bigger than ourselves — and they are. That's what makes them so necessary. They challenge us to reach beyond our current capabilities, fostering personal growth and transformation.

Super big dreamy goals cultivate character, like grit, resilience, and determination. The journey toward realizing them is rarely smooth sailing. It's marked by setbacks, obstacles, and moments of doubt. Yet it's precisely these challenges that test our resolve and fortitude, ultimately strengthening our confidence that we can do whatever feels too big or too scary. We realize that each setback becomes an opportunity to learn, adapt, and persevere, bringing us one step closer to turning our dreams into reality.

Super big dreamy goals serve as catalysts for personal and professional progress. They ignite your imagination, spur innovation, and propel you toward a future limited only by the boundaries of your imagination. Embrace their grandness with warmth and confidence knowing that they hold the power to transform not only your life but the world around you.

Press Play

It's time to press play on those super big dreamy goals by naming them and planning for how you can achieve them. To start, consider the different areas in your life and what super big dreamy goals you might set for them. There is no limit to the number of goals and dreams you can have. Your radiance loves to support all the things that light you up.

Here are some idea generators. Take these and make them your own.

- **Career advancement:** If you want to make a meaningful impact in your career, you might set a goal to reach a leadership position in your organization within a specific time frame or to become a VP or CEO. This goal would help to align with values of growth and contribution, pushing you to expand your skills and influence.
  - What is one super big dreamy goal you could set for your career advancement?

- **Personal development:** If you love continuous learning and self-improvement, you could set a stretch goal to complete a challenging certification or degree program in your field of interest. This would reflect your commitment to growth and align with your dream of becoming an expert in your field.
  - What is one super big dreamy goal you could set for personal development?

- **Health and wellness:** If you desire to prioritize health and well-being, you might set a stretch goal to complete a marathon or achieve a specific fitness milestone, such as running a certain distance or lifting a certain weight. Perhaps you want to focus on increasing your energy levels by improving your nutrition. If so, you might set a stretch goal to eat 80 percent whole foods and 20 percent processed food. Goals like these would align with your desire to prioritize your physical and mental health.

- o What is one super big dreamy goal you could set for health and wellness?

- **Financial independence:** If financial freedom is important to you, set a stretch goal to increase your income or savings by a significant percentage within a set time frame. Maybe you could start a side hustle or invest in real estate; increase your odds of success by doing something you love and making money doing it. Goals like these would align with your values of autonomy and security, driving you to take strategic actions to improve your financial situation.
  - o What is one super big dreamy goal you could set for financial independence?

- **Contribution and service:** If giving back to your community or making a difference in the world lights you up, you might set a stretch goal to start a personal brand that focuses on uplifting others or to volunteer at a nonprofit that resonates with you. Goals like these would support your commitment to service and align with your dream of creating positive change in the world.
  - o What is one super big dreamy goal you could set toward contribution and service?

- **Creativity and self-expression:** If creativity and self-expression are central to your life vision, you could set a stretch goal to launch a new product, start a creative project, or pursue a passion project like writing a book or starting a podcast that pushes the boundaries of your creativity. This would support your desire to express yourself authentically and make a unique contribution to the world.

- o   What is one super big dreamy goal you could set related to your creativity and self-expression?

- **Relationships and connection:** If having meaningful relationships and connection with others is a top priority, you might set a goal to deepen existing relationships or cultivate new ones through more one-on-one time, networking, mentoring, or social activities. This would support your commitment to building strong connections and align with your desire to create a supportive community around you.

- o   What is one super big dreamy goal you could set for creating meaningful relationships and connections?

By setting super big dreamy goals that are aligned with your values and desires, you can pursue ambitious objectives with confidence and conviction, knowing that they resonate deeply with who you are and what you aspire to achieve. This alignment also allows Infinite Intelligence to come in and support you by opening doors and creating new opportunities that did not exist before.

Macro and Micro Goal Setting

As you press play on your super big dreamy goals, a useful tool to help you achieve them is macro and micro goal setting. Macro goal setting looks at the big picture, such as the date by which you'd like to achieve something. Then, with micro goal setting, you define at least three small steps or goals you can do now to help you accomplish them. For example, say someone's macro goal is to launch a podcast by the end of the year. Their three micro goals could be determining podcast theme and style, researching podcasting platforms, and finding a handful of podcasts with similar ideas to help clarify the concept.

Take a moment to focus on one of your super big dreamy goals. In a journal, use the prompts below to name your macro goal and define micro goals related to it. Repeat this process with as many goals as you like. Then, as you start to accomplish the micro goals, keep setting new ones as you continue on the road to achieving your dreams and shining brightly in your radiance.

> Macro goal: What is your super big dreamy goal? When do you want to accomplish it?
>
> Micro goals: What are three actions you could take now that will help you achieve your super big dreamy goal?

The Power of AND

According to surveys, most working professionals (up to 98 percent) are suffering from or on the verge of burnout, and less than a fifth (as low as 17 percent) are actively setting goals. So I suspect that we'd see much less burnout if people gave themselves permission to pursue their career and their dreams outside of work, and if they set goals for each. This is why I recommend, to avoid getting stuck in our UN-potential, that we name and pursue super big dreamy goals for ourselves.

When I reflect on my parents, I've asked myself, "When did they stop dreaming?" My dad got close to being a professionally successful, famous musician, winning a state championship with his country band Southern Star. When the band broke up, he just never really put the same passion back into his music. My mom stopped dreaming of being a rock star by the time I was in middle school. I witnessed her become extremely practical, focusing her efforts on her motherly duties and rarely playing her piano.

Once they both stopped doing the thing that made them happy, their radiance dimmed. Their passion and zest for life all but evaporated. They became disconnected from themselves, their souls, and everything. This disconnection from their truth and passion ultimately led them to abandon who they were over who they settled to be. I learned a valuable lesson from my parents: *It's not accomplishing the super big dreamy goal itself that is important. Rather, the pursuit is what matters most.*

We are all working professionals *and* we are creative marvels longing to express ourselves — whether that's through gardening, decorating, engineering, dancing, singing, playing sports, or something else. That is the Power of AND. Whatever our profession, we do that, and whatever our passion, we do that, too. We don't have to become a rock star or an Olympic gold medalist. The simple act of remaining committed to both our work and our creative selves is the secret to inviting in more purpose, passion, and prosperity.

Why would we ever hit pause on those dreams? That's the million-dollar question I asked myself about my parents. And I've found there are several common reasons why people put their dreams on pause. Take note if any seem familiar to you:

- Fear of failure: To put this in perspective, in terms of what people fear the most, fear of failure ranks higher than the fear of public speaking and the fear of spiders. One out of three people won't even start the pursuit of something because the fear is that strong.
- Self-doubt: This causes us to question our capabilities and shakes our confidence, resulting in procrastination or feeling stuck.
- Commitment to responsibility: Work, bills, and overall responsibilities can eclipse the pursuit of our dreams.
- Prioritizing obligations: Family, whether it's taking care of kids or aging parents, tends to get so prioritized that chasing one's own desires becomes a struggle.
- Fear of judgment: The fear of not being accepted and even rejected is so high that it can feel too risky to pursue dreams that may result in disapproval or criticism.

You have had dreams and goals since you were a child that are longing for you to press play. Ask any kindergartner what they want to be when they grow up, and they confidently name their dreams, from practical to magical. Try telling a five-year-old girl that she can't be a mermaid when she grows up, and she will explain all the ways you are wrong.

In order to press play on your super big dreamy goals, all you have to do is give yourself permission. Is there some creative longing you've wanted to express since you were a kid? When I was eight, I knew I was a writer and speaker, and so did my stuffed animals. I didn't ask anyone's permission or ask anyone else what I should be. I just knew. You know yours, too. Just stop and consider what you ruminated about when you were young. What did you obsess over? What fascinated you?

Invite your imagination and your creativity, and reexplore your super big dreamy goals through the lens of possibility.

Reigniting the Spark

As I say, pursuing your super big dreamy goals doesn't mean abandoning your job. It doesn't mean aiming for the pinnacle of success in a certain field. Super big dreamy goals are more about how we feel and expressing a skill or passion that lights us up. Thinking of it that way, what ignites the spark of your creativity?

Take my friend Erin. She was deep into the world of tech sales and craving a career boost. She wasn't certain if that would mean a role change within or outside her organization. The timing wasn't exactly right to explore possibilities, yet she was feeling an internal nudge for more growth and more passion.

At this same time, just for fun, I had started to make positive affirmation yoga T-shirts. As soon as Erin and I started chatting about my T-shirts, I noticed a twinkle in her eye. Turns out, she enjoys making jewelry. I asked her if she wanted to join me at an upcoming trade show, where I was going to be selling my shirts, and she said yes, eagerly whipping up some bracelets to sell.

Once Erin tapped into her radiant core, her creative mojo shot to the surface. She made those bracelets and strutted her stuff at several trade shows with me, and while I won't claim we were raking in the big bucks, what I can tell you is that Erin was on fire. She had that soul glow, and soon after, with a newfound spark, she landed that career-boosting role she'd been eyeing.

This is what happens when we reconnect with the radiance that dwells within. Perhaps accessing the limitless and creative part inside feels as foreign as going to a new country. Perhaps it's familiar but neglected, or you simply want to access more than you are right now. Here are some ways to reignite that spark:

- Return to your roots: Think back to what set your heart on fire as a young kid. Whether it was music, writing, art, or some other flavor of creative magic, revisiting your roots can help you reconnect with your expansive, creative self.
- Experiment and take risks: Get gutsy! Creativity thrives when we're willing to try new things and break the norm.
- Keep dreaming big: Don't lose sight of those mammoth dreams of yours. Let 'em be your North Star, guiding you beyond limits. Imagine those super big dreamy goals often, and make sure they're packed with meaning and purpose.
- Dance to old tunes: As silly as it sounds, dance to songs that made you move and groove as a kid. This helps to suspend critical thinking. It gives you a moment to connect back with the part of you that is free and unlimited in potential. My go-to is Whitney Houston's "How Will I Know."

As you reconnect with the joyful and magical parts of your childhood when your imagination ran free, pay attention to what comes up. The things that brought you joy as a kid are often clues to the innate strengths, gifts, and talents that make you uniquely you. Your super big dreamy goals will take root and begin to blossom into reality when you reconnect with your uniqueness and give it permission to exist.

Finding what ignites your soul is a journey. There's no one-size-fits-all approach for rekindling your spark. Big dreams don't happen overnight, but they do happen one step at a time. Like Erin, they might involve a career upgrade, or they might mean pursuing an entirely new career. Either way, to bring your super big dreamy goals to life requires doing more of what you love.

Your soul longs to tap into that creative, limitless, and passionate part of yourself. Unleashing your potential is not a linear process. Grant yourself permission to dream big, invite your passions to express themselves through you, and lean into the Power of AND to reignite that spark.

Protecting your potential from sizzling out requires you to break up with burnout, break free from the BS that holds you back, power up your choices, make boundaries your best friend, and give yourself permission to have super big dreamy goals. The more you practice these skills, the more you will rise into the role of CEO of your life. You will take the reins and create a life that you absolutely love!

Grab Your Gemstone: Setting and pursuing super big dreamy goals, by reconnecting with your passions and creativity, helps you live a more fulfilled life. Giving yourself permission to dream big and pursue those dreams, even if they seem daunting or unconventional, will help boost your overall confidence and clarity. Embracing the Power of AND allows you to pursue both your professional career and your personal dreams, leading to a more radiant and purposeful life.

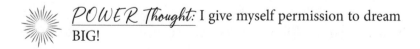

POWER Thought: I give myself permission to dream BIG!

POWER Up Your Practice 5: The Permission Slip

This exercise helps you bring into existence all that you were meant to be and pursue. The act of signing a contract signals to your inner self and Infinite Intelligence that you are committed to unleashing your potential, even if it feels uncomfortable. The Universe will then conspire in your favor not only to support you but to open the doors to unlimited possibilities.

Read and sign the permission slip below to ignite your super big dreamy goals and bring them to life. Or if you wish, copy these two pages, sign the slip, and keep it where you can see it. Or write and sign your own permission slip, phrasing your pledge in whatever way is meaningful to you.

I hereby grant myself full permission to pursue my super big dreamy goals unapologetically. I acknowledge that my dreams are valid, worthy, and within my reach. I recognize that I am deserving of success, abundance, and fulfillment in all areas of my life.

I understand that pursuing my dreams may require courage, resilience, and perseverance. However, I am committed to facing any challenges that may arise with unwavering determination and optimism.

I give myself permission to embrace my uniqueness, talents, and passions fully. I will not dim my light or hold back out of fear of judgment or failure. I release any self-limiting beliefs or doubts that may have held me back in the past. From this moment forward, I choose to believe in myself and my ability to achieve greatness.

I understand that my dreams may evolve over time, and that is OK. I give myself permission to adapt, pivot, and explore new opportunities along my journey. I commit to taking inspired action toward my goals each day, no matter how small or daunting the steps may seem. I trust that each action I take brings me closer to realizing my dreams.

I pledge to celebrate my progress, milestones, and achievements along the way. I will cultivate a mindset of gratitude and self-love, recognizing my worthiness of success and joy. By signing this permission slip, I affirm my commitment to pursuing my super big dreamy goals unapologetically. I am ready to step into my power, unleash my potential, and create the life of my dreams.

And so it is.

Signature:
Date:

PART TWO

OWN YOUR

Opportunities

When something I can't control happens, I ask myself:
Where is the hidden gift, where is the positive in this?

— SARA BLAKELY, Founder of Spanx

CHAPTER SIX

Change Your Meaning, Change Your Life

*D*id you know that the meaning you give to your experiences influences the quality of your life? You have the power within to consciously shift and shape the meaning of past and present events to a higher-quality emotion, which then positively shapes your life. In other words, *changing your meaning will change your life.*

Within the POWER Method, part 1 discusses the importance of protecting our potential and how to do so, and part 2 explores how to overcome obstacles and turn them into opportunities by taking ownership of outcomes. This chapter examines how the meaning we assign to events and experiences impacts the trajectory of our lives. By cultivating awareness of the meaning we assign to what happens in our lives, we can decide whether this meaning supports or sabotages us and our dreams.

Still Standing

"Ladies," I said to an audience of women leaders, "let me see you stand tall if you've ever lost a loved one. Stay standing. Stand strong if you've faced cancer or any life-altering disease. Rise if you've walked through the storm of divorce. Stand proud if you've worn the superhero cape of a single mom. Finally, stand unapologetically if you know the all-too-familiar pain of getting laid off or working at a toxic job."

From the stage, I scanned the sea of incredible women before me, not a soul seated. Every one of them was a warrior in her own right. I invited them to look around the room to visually experience the magnitude of the strength and resilience that was standing in the room. "Give yourself a round of applause ladies because you are still standing," I said. In that moment, you could feel their energy shift from feeling ashamed of their trials to feeling empowered by their triumphs.

Just like these ladies, you have withstood the various storms of life and are still standing. Whether it be losing a loved one, struggling with addictions, toxic and abusive relationships, bankruptcy, severe health issues, or anything else, you have weathered the storm. Your friends and family have, too. No one is exempt from stormy seasons. Yet every storm has something valuable to teach us — from strengthening our character to learning what to avoid to discovering helpful habits that support our fullest potential.

As you reflect on some of the stormy seasons of your life and the experiences you've weathered, and yet are still standing, what comes up for you? How have these storms strengthened your character? What qualities now shine as a result? What have you learned from them and how does that lesson serve you now? Lastly, how do you show up positively to support yourself and others differently?

This reminds me of an anonymous quote: "Fate whispered to the warrior, 'You will never withstand the storm.' The warrior whispered back, 'I am the storm.'" You are stronger than you may be giving yourself credit for. If you shift the meaning you've given to the storms in your life, so they represent how they have helped you rather than how they have hurt you, those storms will empower you.

Meaning-Making Machines

Humans by nature are meaning-making machines. Something happens — good or bad — and boom, we assign meaning to it.

Without knowing it, we are preprogrammed to see patterns and connections and to create explanations where there are gaps. This helps us make sense of life and our place within it.

There are various reasons we seek meaning in events. Assigning meaning helps regulate our emotions. It defines our role in a situation and impacts our self-concept, either providing reassurance and self-confidence or self-doubt and feelings of inadequacy.

When we identify as the hero in our storyline, we are resourceful. Problem-solving, goal-pursuit, and adaptiveness become our strengths. Yet if we are the villain or victim in our story, then we fall into behaviors such as avoidance, rumination, and self-loathing.

Our energy, our emotions, and our thoughts become our living reality. The meaning we assign to the happenings around us influences the quality of our energy, emotions, and thoughts. The quality of these elements creates the quality of our lives.

This is why it's so important to take ownership of your perceptions, challenge yourself, and find the gift in what you have been through. After all, you are the CEO of your life, and you get to dictate what the quality of your life looks and feels like.

The Frequency of Emotions

Emotions have frequency just like radio waves. The higher the frequency, the more radiant you are. The lower the frequency, the deeper you fall in your zone of UN-potential. To simplify, emotions fall into one of two buckets — radiant emotions or zone of UN-potential emotions. Feeling radiant emotions more often and regularly will make life more fulfilling. The more your emotions hang out in the zone of UN-potential, the greater the sense of disconnection and frustration you will feel.

Here is a quick look at the two buckets of emotions and what each contains. The zone of UN-potential emotions ends with the lowest-frequency ones.

Radiant Emotions

- Love
- Freedom
- Empowerment
- Joy
- Passion
- Faith / positive expectations
- Appreciation
- Enthusiasm/excitement
- Eagerness
- Happiness
- Courage
- Hopefulness
- Playfulness
- Resilience
- Contentment

Zone of UN-potential Emotions

- Restlessness/boredom
- Frustration
- Anxiety/worry
- Doubt
- Discouragement
- Insecurity
- Indecision
- Blame
- Anger
- Grief
- Disconnection/depression
- Unworthiness
- Shame
- Guilt
- Fear

The meaning we ascribe to events impacts our emotional charge, which affects everything we do. Our emotions can either serve us or sabotage us.

For example, if we constantly ruminate on a past experience, and more than half the time we are feeling low-frequency emotions in the zone of UN-potential, our low-level emotions could sabotage our future. On the other hand, if we are chasing super big dreamy goals and we constantly envision an awesome future, we begin to embody radiant emotions. When we spend more than half our time in radiant emotions, especially the high-frequency ones, our emotions serve us. We unleash our potential and our life starts to unfold in the most beautiful and unexpected ways.

Consider my bathroom-floor moment. Everyone experiences something like that at some point. Symbolically, that image of crying on the bathroom floor is wrapped in fear, grief, desperation, despair, and powerlessness. These feelings kept me in my zone of UN-potential. That was one of the lowest emotional points of my life. My energy, thoughts, and emotions were wildly disempowering.

When you are having a bathroom-floor moment, take ownership of your reaction and shift your perspective. The moment I realized I was the CEO of my life, a wave of empowerment surged through me. I rose off the ground a different woman than the one who went down. Why? Because I shifted what that moment meant about me and my future. When I rose, I made a quantum leap from the lowest emotions to some of the highest ones, including hopefulness, optimism, empowerment, enthusiasm, and passion — all in a matter of minutes. This experience changed the trajectory of my life forever.

This level of profound change is available for everyone. I have seen countless leaders, high performers, and lofty dreamers receive the most remarkable outcomes and reach outlandish goals as a result of changing their meaning. When you embrace knowing that your emotions impact your thoughts and energy, and that collectively these three elements — emotions, thoughts, and energy — are responsible for shaping the quality of your life, you'll feel empowered to change your life in the most magnificent ways.

Changing Your Meaning

Meaning has the power to break us down and to build us up. If you find yourself in the lower subset of emotions, know that you can use this as an opportunity to power up your choices. You get to choose what experiences mean to you and what they say about you.

Changing the meaning you give to something can be a powerful way to shift your perspective and improve your overall life. Once you change your meaning to a more positive one, you will experience more higher-frequency emotions. When this happens consistently, life as well as the Universe supports you in the direction of your potential.

Here are some practical ways to change your meaning:

- Practice reframing: When faced with a challenging situation or negative thought, consciously reframe it in a more positive or empowering light. For example, instead of seeing failure as a setback, view it as an opportunity to learn and grow.

- Challenge negative beliefs: Identify any negative beliefs or assumptions you hold about yourself or the world around you and challenge them with evidence to the contrary. This can help you adopt a more balanced and realistic perspective. For example, if you think you aren't smart enough, think of times when you used your smarts to achieve something or to help someone else.

- Seek alternative interpretations: When faced with a situation that you perceive negatively, consider alternative interpretations or explanations that may be more positive or neutral. This can help avoid jumping to conclusions and assuming the worst. For example, let's say that your best friend didn't call you back when they said they would, and you assumed you must have done something wrong. Instead, assume positive intent and be confident that your friendship is of value to both of you.

- Surround yourself with positivity: Surround yourself with positive influences, whether supportive friends and family, uplifting media, or inspiring books and podcasts. This can help reinforce positive beliefs and attitudes, making it easier to change the meaning you give to things.
- Seek professional help: If you're struggling to change your meaning on your own, consider seeking support from a therapist or counselor. They can provide guidance and techniques tailored to your specific needs and challenges.

As you consider the role your emotions, thoughts, and energy play in the quality of your life, you can choose at any time to change the meaning and change your life.

Grab Your Gemstone: The meanings you assign to your experiences have a profound influence on the quality of your life. By consciously shifting and shaping this meaning, you have the power to transform past and present events into sources of empowerment and growth. Understanding the frequency of emotions and the role they play in shaping your reality is crucial, as higher-frequency emotions lead to a more fulfilled and happy life.

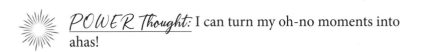

POWER Thought: I can turn my oh-no moments into ahas!

POWER Up Your Practice 6: Question and Reframe

While we are not always responsible for what happens to us, the good news is that we are responsible for how we respond going forward. Consider this journal prompt exercise your safe zone for personal exploration and transformation.

In a journal or notebook, question and reframe meanings that need a positive twist: The simple act of answering these questions and reframing your perspective signals to the Universe that you are open and want change. The Universe in turn will respond to support you.

Question and reframe: To start questioning old thoughts, ask yourself: Are they even legit? Are these thoughts hard facts or is it possible that they are a story? How could you shift these to empowering thoughts? Then challenge them! Reframe those negative emotions into powerful, uplifting beliefs. Use these questions as guides:

- What strengths do I now have as a result of what I've experienced?
- How has this happened for me rather than to me?
- What gifts has this situation given me?
- In what ways has this positively shaped me into the person I am today?
- What positive meanings can I give to a past event that supports me going forward? How can I take what I've learned and help someone else?

Use the magic of the written word to change the quality of your meanings to positively change the quality of your life. With each word you write, you're harnessing your power, shining brighter, and showing the Universe who's boss!

Remember, you can download the complimentary Return to Radiance Personal Transformation Guide, which includes all the POWER Up Your Practice exercises as well as some radiant extras, at Resources.ReturnToRadianceBook.com.

CHAPTER SEVEN

Align with Your Values

*I*n a study on emotional intelligence and self-awareness published in the *Harvard Business Review*, researchers estimated that only 10 to 15 percent of people have internal self-awareness. Someone with self-awareness has a pretty good understanding of their values, beliefs, and passions, as well as the roles they play in enhancing their life. Our values play a crucial role in our life because emotion and belief are tied to them, and they guide how we assign meaning to events.

This chapter explores the role that values play in your life and helps you discover and become aware of the values that are most meaningful to you. Without self-awareness, our values can lead us astray. We may find ourselves making choices that we think make sense but for some reason or another don't end up working quite the way we thought. Knowing our values and the role they play in our lives will help us own the opportunities that come our way with more clarity and confidence.

The Role Values Play

Values are so important; they impact and influence so much of what we do. Personally, I had never considered the role values played in my life until I took my first values assessment.

Here are some of the key roles values play and the positive influence they can have on your life:

- Identity: Your values reflect who you are and what you stand for. They shape you and contribute to an increased sense of self-esteem, self-worth, and belonging. Living by your values helps to create a positive self-image.
- Guidance: They help you navigate life's complexities. They provide you with a moral compass and help direct your behavior to what you consider right or important.
- Decision-making: Values provide a framework and something to base your decisions on. They help prioritize options, so you choose the best course of action, one that is consistent with your beliefs and goals and what matters to you most.
- Belonging: Shared values form the basis of meaningful relationships in every context. When values are shared, it cultivates trust, cohesion, and mutual respect. This leads to a deeper sense of belonging and fosters innovation and teamwork.

Our values influence everything from our decisions to who we associate with to our self-identity. This is a pretty big deal! Values take a lot of space in the overall makeup of who we are.

The more you align with your values, the more you feel authentic. From this place, you have more clarity and confidence to pursue those super big dreamy goals and to do so leaning into your strengths, gifts, and talents. Your radiance brightens and expands, clearing the way for more impact.

Values Have Two Sides

Just like a coin, values have two sides. One side supports you and the other side sabotages you. Values themselves don't have any intent or motive, but the meaning you assign to them does. It's not uncommon for a value to lead us in a rogue direction if we are unaware that the value exists and the meaning that we are subconsciously giving it overrides other important areas of our life. The same goes for having an undercover value that is subconsciously working for us because it's prioritized well in our life — things may seem to work in our favor a lot more.

Have you ever been labeled a workaholic by your family and friends? I know I have. Quite a few times. I have always loved to work. It's a place for me to pursue my passion. I can be part of a team, contribute to something bigger, and if things go really well, I get to make a positive impact on my clients, my teammates, the company, and my family. I truly feel that my work matters.

Does your work matter to you, too? If so, *meaningful work* may be a top value of yours, as it is for me. The thing is, I didn't learn that it was a top value of mine until 2020, after I took a values assessment. As soon as I identified *meaningful work* as a top value for me, so many things made sense. First, I celebrated. Thinking to myself, *Awesome, I'm not a workaholic. My work is just important to me.* Then I reflected on how much this value has also been a silent saboteur because I was unaware of it.

Back in 2016, I left my role as a regional sales manager with Dell Technologies to pursue a leadership role outside of my industry because the new company's motto was "Putting People First." I have a similar leadership mantra of "People Before Profits." What I know now that I didn't know then is that *meaningful work* is one of my top three values along with *family* and *appreciation*. The pull to this new job was so strong, and my role felt so important, that I even took a pay cut.

I was so committed and loyal to this value of meaningful work that I sacrificed my own finances, time with my family, and my well-being in pursuit of what I thought mattered to me. While my work in this job was meaningful, it did not align with my other two top values: family and appreciation. It's a great big world and there are other meaningful jobs that would have aligned better.

Fast-forward to today: I am still doing work that feels

meaningful, and my career and my finances are flowing. Plus, my health is also thriving, passion is alive within me, and I get to spend time with my family and even include them in some of my work adventures. I can feel the appreciation for the work I do. Now I am aligned with my top three values. I feel connected to myself and others. I still work hard, but everything I do fills me up and replenishes me — and this is what I want for you!

My story is an example of how one value can play a significant role in our life, one that can either serve us or sabotage us depending on our level of awareness. To truly own your opportunities, aligning with your values is a complete game changer.

Values for Victory

Values are very personal and differ from person to person — very rarely do two people share the same exact value pattern. If you want to improve your performance, outcomes, and goals, using values as your asset will help guide you to do just that. It's also important to recognize if you are out of alignment with your values, since that will show up in your work, your homelife, or both.

Here's another example. I once worked with a top performer who named *wealth* as a top value. This made sense because her ability to constantly overachieve was tied to that value. She grew up without a lot of money and was trying to change the generational story for herself and her family. However, she named *health* and *freedom* as her other top three values, and her focus on wealth was compromising her well-being to the point that she would forget to eat. Her anxiety and stress levels were extremely high, impacting her mental and emotional well-being. She was burning out. She knew it, her team knew it, and her leader knew it, but no one knew why.

When I talked to her, it became clear that her health had been deprioritized due to her overattachment to wealth. Because health was an important value to her, the fact that she wasn't giving her health attention was causing her more stress. And even though more wealth might eventually fulfill her desire for freedom, the dedication required to make money was leaving her no room for freedom and adventure. Her leader was concerned that if she didn't do something to avoid burnout, her performance might suffer or even worse she would quit.

After reviewing her top values and making a plan to honor all of them, she made some changes. She began to take lunch breaks, and she walked during some of her phone meetings rather than sitting. She gave herself permission to do a new activity once or twice a month. Within a couple months, this top performer was back in her radiance and breaking new sales records. The coolest part about this story is that wealth skyrocketed as a result of her prioritizing her other values of health and freedom. The goal is to align with our values so that they are a source of energy and passion lighting the way for our most victorious outcomes.

Do you know what your own top values are? Use this chapter's exercise to recognize them so you can avoid their pitfalls, align your work, surround yourself with the right people, and make decisions reflecting your truth and what matters most to you. How awesome would this make you feel? In what ways could you leverage your values to up-level your life?

Imagine knowing the values of your teammates or even your family members. How could knowing what is meaningful to them help foster a better relationship? Or even contribute to their overall performance and well-being? The possibilities for using values for victory are endless!

Grab Your Gemstone: Values serve various roles, including shaping identity, providing guidance, influencing decision-making, and fostering a sense of belonging. However, values have two sides: They can either support or sabotage you based on your level of awareness and how you prioritize them. Ultimately, understanding and leveraging values can lead to greater authenticity, fulfillment, and achievement in your life.

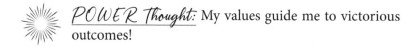

POWER Thought: My values guide me to victorious outcomes!

POWER Up Your Practice 7: Your Top Values

The goal of this exercise is to help you discover and name your most important values. First, review the values named in the word cloud below. Take a moment to really feel each value. Then when you feel ready, choose (or circle) your top ten, in any order. If one of your top ten values isn't named here, add it to your list.

Love   Variety   Discipline   Appreciation   Adventure
Certainty   Meaningful work   Health   Pleasure
Trust   Control   Respect   Challenge
Privacy   Security   Family   Peace   Compassion
Passion   Creativity   Fame
Forgiveness   Determination   Reputation
Religion   Wisdom
Growth   Job security   Ethics
Courage   Justice   Tradition
Ambition   Acceptance   Competence
Tolerance   Equality   Freedom
Helpfulness   Popularity   Wealth
Beauty   Contribution
Success   Financial security   Authority   Influence
Inner harmony   Loyalty   Excellence   Honesty
Authenticity   Spirituality
Intelligence   Accountability
Friendship   Independence   Curiosity
Commitment
Teamwork   Uniqueness   Excitement

After choosing your top ten, reflect on which of these are your top three core values, the ones that resonate with you the most. In a journal, write those down, and then explore the potential strengths and setbacks of each one. For each value, describe the strengths or why it matters to you, describe the potential pitfalls or possible negative consequences of that value, and then consider any aha realizations that this reflection generates. How can you use this value to navigate decision-making and improve your choices in all aspects of your life?

If you are craving a deeper dive into understanding your values, visit one of my favorite free websites for an assessment: Personal Values Assessment (https://personalvalu.es). I have no affiliation with this company. I have used them in the past and have been happy with their outcomes.

CHAPTER EIGHT

Shine Brighter Than Your Doubts

This quote by Suzy Kassem just about sums up this chapter's issue: "Doubt kills more dreams than failure ever will." Doubt stops us before we even start because it doesn't like failure. Doubt can even be tricky. It can show up as positive traits like overpreparedness. But researching something extensively might really be a form of procrastination that reflects doubt. Despite how powerful doubt can feel, it can never completely diminish our magnificence. It can only dull it until we learn to shine brighter than it.

When you start taking steps in the direction of your super big dreamy goals and of your full potential, you can be sure doubts will surface. Personal transformation is full of new beginnings and new ways of thinking. While it's exciting to dream about what's possible and to take action to bring it into reality, it also stirs up a lot of uncertainty and doubt.

Know this: You can choose to overcome doubt the same way you choose to change the meaning of past events and experiences. Doubt impacts your future because it's filled with false narratives that prevent you from taking action. Remember, it hates failure.

Your radiance is a brilliant and expansive force filled with gifts, talents, and strengths to outshine doubt even on the most paralyzing day. This chapter describes how to lessen doubt's impact on your life. Ultimately, doubt can be transformed into self-assurance and provide a refreshing boost of self-confidence.

More Feared Than Ghosts!

According to a survey by the social network Linkagoal, one of every three people is afraid of failure. In fact, the fear of failure was higher than the fear of spiders and of ghosts. So if you ever fear failure, you have a lot of company.

People openly talk about their fears of spiders and ghosts along with justifications for their fears: "Spiders are creepy. They have eight legs. What's to like about them?" And "Ghosts are scary as hell. I don't want to talk to a dead person. That's a no for me." Even when people joke about their fears, it's easy to understand that they are still afraid. We accept it, honor it, and move on.

That's not what happens with the fear of failure, though. People don't talk about their fear of failure, and it's rare to joke about it. Why is this? I think it's because shame is tied to failure, and shame is something that most people are subconsciously programmed to hide. We never want to reveal our weaknesses, our inefficiencies, and our imperfections. These could bring shame to ourselves and our families. That might sound extreme, but in severe cases, it's true. Shame believes the worst thing that could ever happen when it comes to failing is being made fun of or being perceived as less than perfect. That's where doubt can come in to save the day.

I believe that if doubt could look in the mirror, it would see itself as a superhero, one that protects us from all the possible harm that could come our way. If doubt stops us from going into uncharted waters, then we can't die, hurt ourselves, or make a fool of ourselves. Doubt's job is done and another day is saved.

But does doubt save us? Doubt might prevent failure, but not trying new things prevents progress. At best, doubt has good intentions, since it is simply trying to keep us alive. What doubt doesn't do is allow us to thrive.

Knowing that failure is part of personal growth allows you to focus more on what you can learn from acknowledging doubt's existence and choosing to do something anyway. This provides an opportunity to sharpen your skills and use the amazing gifts, strengths, and talents that are part of your radiance. This mindset allows you to shine brighter than your doubts.

You Already Are

Michelle, one of my former account managers and top performers, was visibly upset when she said, "Becca, I can't step up for that promotion. Others have so much more experience than me. Plus, I'm bound to just screw it up."

I knew something deeper was going on with her and wouldn't let that slide, so I pressed her, "Why aren't you excited about this promotion? You've wanted to advance your career for the last year." She avoided my question, so I said to her, "C'mon now, you know I'm going to support you either way, so let's hear it."

Finally, she broke her silence. "I'm a single mom who had to drop out of college. It feels like everyone here is more qualified than me," she confessed. Aha, doubt was trying to come in to save the day! Michelle had spun a story in her mind, convinced that being a single mom and college dropout somehow equaled her not being good enough. So I probed further and asked, "Why does that make you a nonviable candidate for this promotion?" She said, "If I couldn't keep a marriage or finish college, how can I lead a team?" My response to her was, "You already are."

The truth was, the team already saw Michelle as a leader and advisor. Not because she was trying to be. She was seen this way because that was how she showed up. She embodied the very thing she thought she wasn't capable of. Her radiance was working in her favor and she didn't even realize it. Sometimes your gifts, talents, and strengths are so native and natural that you might dismiss them as not that big of a deal — and doubt creeps in. They are, however, a very big deal and can serve as your catalysts to living a fulfilling and rewarding life.

It took further conversation, more questions, and some self-reflection for Michelle to let go of the grip that doubt had on her. Eventually, she felt confident enough to apply for the promotional role and bring her A game to the interview. She successfully placed as the top candidate and got the promotion.

But she almost didn't. Doubt was afraid to let her fail. That fear would have prevented Michelle from progressing in life and in her career. Michelle had to shine brighter than her doubt so that she could continue to elevate and evolve. Like Michelle, you are capable of shining brighter than your doubts.

When was the last time doubt surfaced for you and you didn't let it hold you back? How did that make you feel? What did you learn as a result?

Fact or Fiction

To overcome doubt, an amazing tool is to play a little game I call Fact or Fiction. Naturally, humans are storytellers, especially when it comes to ourselves. When there is an information gap, we want to fill it. Sometimes we create a false narrative around a past event or experience or about what might happen in the future. These false narratives are fictional because they are not rooted in anything factual. They are rooted in assumptions.

Michelle, like many of us, got tangled in a web of doubt because of a story she was telling herself: *College dropout, divorced — something's wrong with me. I'm just not cut out for success.* This is an example of where a little game of Fact or Fiction can help create a new empowered perspective. In Michelle's case, it helped her decide to apply for the promotion. Here's how it worked:

- Fact or Fiction: Was Michelle a college dropout? Fact; she did drop out of college.
- Fact or Fiction: Was Michelle divorced? Fact; she had recently divorced.

- Fact or Fiction: Was something inherently wrong with Michelle? Fiction; dropping out of college and getting a divorce were choices based on circumstances. These experiences might have caused pain, and Michelle might feel she could have made better choices, but neither equates to being a bad leader and not being cut out for success. Those are self-defeating assumptions she made about herself, which is why I label them as fiction.

You can use this same methodology to examine any narratives that may be allowing doubt to prevent you from taking action. This will help you fail forward for your greater good versus playing it safe and staying stagnant. Know this — you have the power to rewrite your narrative and create a new story. You've got to shine a spotlight on the stories you tell yourself to discover whether they are fact or fiction.

Doubt-Busting Questions

Doubt denies dreams because it often feels like intuition. Intuition is usually defined as the ability to understand something immediately, without the need for conscious reasoning. It's a form of knowledge or understanding that comes from within, rather than through external sources or deliberate thought. It's super important to learn how to discern doubt from intuition because they sometimes feel the same. Doubt is rooted in the assumption that something is going to go wrong or will not be worth the effort — it gives an intense feeling of no. Intuition is rooted in Infinite Intelligence, and when it gives a strong feeling of no, it's partnered with an inner knowing that something isn't right.

Using doubt-busting questions is another great tool that helps you discern the difference between the two. Once you get good at uncovering the narrative you created using doubt-busting questions, it makes playing Fact or Fiction a lot easier. Both tools are meant to help you take action in the direction of your super big dreamy goals. If you don't, unrealized dreams and desires will dull your shine and contribute to disconnection from yourself, your radiance, and the Universe.

Questions shine a light on your doubt narratives and stories. They help you figure out how your thoughts and feelings impact your actions and goals. Good questions find holes in your assumptions and allow you to create newer, empowering stories that make you feel like the superstar you are. They also help you strengthen the connection between you and your intuition because each time you dispel doubt, you make room for your intuition to have a stronger relationship with you. You become more self-assured, which allows you to trust yourself more.

Here are ten doubt-busting questions to help you shine brighter than your doubt. As you answer them, be honest with yourself. You'll be surprised how much isn't true and how much your light deserves to shine. Once you are done answering the questions, you are in a great position to play a round of Fact or Fiction. These techniques will help you say no to doubt and yes to your dreams.

Ten Doubt-Busting Questions

1. What narrative am I telling myself right now?
2. Who and where did this story originate from?
3. How does this story make me feel about myself?
4. What does this story prevent me from doing or achieving?
5. Is there any real proof to back up this narrative, or is it just made up to fill in gaps of information?
6. What have I made this mean about myself?
7. How is this story sabotaging and disempowering me?
8. What would someone else say about the narrative I'm telling myself?

9. What's a better story I can tell myself instead? How would this new story serve and empower me?

10. What actions can I take to make this new narrative a reality?

With multiple questions, you get the opportunity to own your outcomes and rewrite your story. Then you can start telling yourself cooler stories, boosting your confidence, and feeling like the fierce one you are. Practice asking yourself a combination of these questions. That's how you up your self-esteem and feel more resilient and sparkly inside.

The truth is we possess a wide range of qualities, both positive and negative. These qualities are inherent in all of us and are part of our human experience. As we explore doubt, we learn it's the meaning and interpretation we attach to our self-limiting stories that keep us motionless. At the end of the day, we are all the things — the good, the bad, the ugly, and the freakin' brilliant. Every single one of us. So don't let doubt steal your dreams. You are destined to shine brightly!

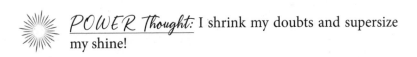 *Grab Your Gemstone:* Doubt rather than failure is more of a significant barrier to your success. Embracing personal transformation, you can overcome doubt by changing your perception of past events and recognizing the false narratives that doubt creates about your future. The more you can bust up doubt, the more self-assured you become. Your confidence increases and allows your talents and strengths to shine, overcoming the paralysis caused by doubt.

POWER Thought: I shrink my doubts and supersize my shine!

POWER Up Your Practice 8: Fact or Fiction

This exercise is designed to help you separate the feelings of doubt from your intuitive insights, using the Fact or Fiction approach. This guides you through questioning your immediate reactions to situations, decisions, or beliefs, allowing you to distinguish between what is rooted in fact and what is influenced by doubt or fear.

Grab your journal, or another medium of choice, and work through this exercise.

1. Identify a situation: Think of a recent situation where you felt torn between following your gut feelings and succumbing to doubt. This could be a decision you needed to make, an opportunity you were considering, or an impulse to start or stop doing something.

2. Describe your feelings: Write down the feelings and thoughts that came up during this situation. Clearly distinguish between what you believe was your intuition speaking and what felt like doubt.

3. Use the Fact or Fiction approach: For each thought or feeling, ask yourself, "Is this a fact or fiction?" Write your thoughts and feelings down first. Then write "fact" or "fiction" next to it. Remember, facts are statements that can be proven true or are inherently true because of your experience. Facts are objective and verifiable. Meanwhile, statements based on assumptions, fears, external opinions, or any form of self-doubt are fictions. Fictions are subjective and often not grounded in reality.

4. Challenge the fictions: Look at each item you've labeled as "fiction." Ask yourself why you believe these statements, where they come from, and what evidence exists that they are not true. This step is crucial for challenging and overcoming doubt.

5. Reinforce the facts: Review the items labeled as "fact." Reflect on how these truths support your intuitive feelings and how acknowledging these facts can guide you toward trusting your intuition more.

6. Reflect on your insights: Next, reflect on what you've learned as a result of this exercise. Consider how the facts support your intuition and how identifying fictions can help mitigate unfounded doubts.

7. List action steps: Finally, write down at least one actionable step you can take based on your intuitive insights, now reinforced by recognizing the facts. This could be a small action toward a decision you've been postponing or a change in how you approach similar situations in the future.

After completing the exercise, take a few moments to reflect on the process and any new understandings you have gained. Recognizing the difference between doubt and intuition can empower you to make decisions more confidently and align your actions with your true self.

Keep practicing this exercise with different situations to strengthen your ability to discern between doubt and intuition. Use the framework of Fact or Fiction to shine brightly in all your awesomeness.

CHAPTER NINE

Turn Strengths into Superpowers

*H*ave you ever obsessed over your weaknesses? Most people have. But have you ever obsessed over your strengths? Most people don't spend much time turning their strengths into superpowers, but that is crucial in your journey to return to radiance and in your ability to own your opportunities going forward.

In my twenty years of corporate leadership experience, I have seen the hyperfocus on weaknesses from annual performance reviews to weekly one-on-ones. Masked in "the spirit of growth," this hyperfocus on what is wrong with us rather than what is right is a leading cause of the disconnection we have with ourselves, our soul, and everyone around us. This critical lens can lead us to withdraw, isolate, and inhibit our action-taking due to a lowered self-image. The cost of this is a decline in personal performance.

On the other hand, focusing on our strengths can result in improved health, overall fulfillment, and increased passion. This positive reinforcement can lead us to greater confidence, creative ideas, and taking calculated risks due to a better self-image. This approach results in increased performance and our ability to reach our super big dreamy goals.

Imagine If...

Gallup, an American multinational analytics and advisory company, offers a self-assessment tool called CliftonStrengths (see Gallup.com/CliftonStrengths) that employees can use to improve their job performance. Over thirty-two million people have tried it, and the data have revealed some incredible organizational results for corporations that focus on strengths:

- 81 percent lower absenteeism
- 64 percent fewer safety incidents
- 41 percent fewer defects (quality)
- 14 percent higher productivity
- 10 percent higher customer ratings
- 18 percent higher sales
- 23 percent higher profitability

These results are more than just great news for companies; this is great news for you. The personal benefits of focusing on your strengths include improved health, stronger relationships, higher levels of fulfillment, and more. So much is gained from focusing on your strengths, gifts, and talents.

Imagine if we lived in a world where from the moment we were born we were encouraged to develop our strengths, gifts, and talents. How different would the world be? How different would our lives be?

This wouldn't stop life's adversities and setbacks from happening. But it sure would help us to turn inward knowing that within lies the answers and our ability to overcome and thrive. In addition, it would set us up societally to help individuals nurture and develop the skills most natural to them, resulting in stronger intuition, confidence, and self-worth.

This is a lovely what-if scenario, but individually, all we can truly focus on is ourselves and the immediate world around us.

Massive outer change starts with massive inner change. If you are being called to make a difference, create positive change, impact the world in some way, or spread more joy — then start getting to know your strengths, talents, and gifts and incorporating them into your life.

Similar but Different

The qualities of strengths, gifts, and talents are similar but different. Understanding the subtle nuances can help your personal growth, so that you harness your innate and developed capacities. Let's explore the individual essences and collective synergy of strengths, gifts, and talents, shedding light on the roles they play in the journey of self-actualization and skill refinement.

STRENGTHS

- Meaning: Strengths are a blend of acquired skills and deepened knowledge, meticulously crafted and polished through persistent effort and time. This process of cultivation allows you to transform raw potential into refined abilities, showcasing the power of dedication in personal and professional growth.
- Characteristics: Typically, strengths reveal themselves in the steadiness of performing tasks and interacting with others. These qualities are tangible and manifest in areas where an individual demonstrates remarkable aptitude and consistent excellence. It's in these arenas of repeated success that your strengths become visible, offering a clear showcase of where your capabilities truly shine.
- Development: Although certain strengths may be rooted in innate talents or gifts, their true blossoming is the result of application, experience, and dedication, when you use time and resources to develop them. This nurturing process is essential in transforming your potential into a palpable skill, taking it from an inherent ability to a mastered craft.

GIFTS

- Meaning: We are all born with a set of capabilities and aptitudes that we effortlessly carry within us. They are part of our essence and our uniqueness. It's not uncommon to dismiss gifts as nothing special because they come so easily to us that we assume everyone must have them as well. This is simply not true. You have unique gifts that when acknowledged and nurtured can flourish into remarkable outcomes and contributions with ease, grace, and joy.

- Characteristics: Gifts frequently make their presence known at a young age. They might show up as genius-level intelligence, creative mastery in art, or a deep empathy and understanding for life. Much like a seed holds the promise of a flower, these natural gifts await cultivation to bloom fully into their most vibrant potential.
- Development: Gifts serve as the initial platform for your potential to shine bright. A supportive environment, positive reinforcement, and ample opportunities to delve into and refine these gifts are critical for your growth.

TALENTS

- Meaning: Talents are predispositions toward particular pursuits. They carry a more defined and targeted nature. Talents are the unrefined gems within us, holding the promise of becoming profound areas of expertise. They are the initial sparks of potential that, through development and dedication, can illuminate a path to remarkable achievements and contributions.
- Characteristics: Talents are often observable in a person's desires and interests from childhood up until the present. They could be in sports, music, math, business, and so on. Your natural-born talents are like signs pointing in the direction of your potential, passion, and purpose.
- Development: Talents require a process of refinement and dedicated practice to evolve into dependable assets. It's through this disciplined approach and persistent

application that talents mature into capabilities that can be called upon reliably and effectively, transforming innate potential into tangible excellence.

Turn Your Strengths into Superpowers

The journey to transform your strengths, talents, and gifts into superpowers requires a holistic and intentional approach that intertwines self-discovery, intention, practice, and ongoing personal development. By identifying what naturally resonates with you, what sparks joy, and where your passions lie, you lay the groundwork for a fulfilling life.

Development of these innate abilities not only elevates your emotional well-being but also aligns you with the vibrations of abundance and prosperity. Aligning your life's endeavors with your strengths facilitates a flow state, reducing stress and enhancing life's harmony.

Investing in yourself, whether through coaching, building a supportive community, or acquiring essential tools, marks a significant step toward realizing your potential. Mastery is not merely about practicing your craft; it's about integrating your gifts into your very essence, transforming your activities into extensions of yourself. Adaptability ensures that your strengths remain a core part of your identity and are resilient through life's ebbs and flows.

Creating and sharing your work allows your strengths to truly become superpowers, influencing and inspiring others. As you continuously evolve and integrate your talents into your life's work, you're not just developing your skills; you're cocreating with the Universe — embracing infinite possibilities. This journey of growth, adaptation, and creativity evolves who you are, inviting you to live in a constant state of exploration and evolution.

What if no restrictions or barriers held you back? How could you leverage your strengths as superpowers? How would they make your life different? What impact would it have on your business? How would you feel?

Here are eight steps for turning your strengths into superpowers. As you contemplate the questions in each one, write your answers and thoughts in a journal.

> **Step 1: Identify.** Begin by understanding what you are naturally good at and how it makes you feel. This could involve self-reflection, feedback from others, or even formal assessments (I recommend Gallup Clifton-Strengths, Gallup.com/CliftonStrengths). Next, consider: What are your natural-born talents and gifts? What are you passionate about? What brings you joy?

> **Step 2: Develop.** Once you identify your gifts, talents, and strengths, develop those that bring you the deepest sense of passion and joy. This isn't about making money; this is about raising your emotional frequency. The more you develop your strengths, the more joy, passion, and fulfillment you will feel, and the more likely you are to align with the frequency of abundance and prosperity. For now, just have fun doing the things that you love! What are some ideas or ways to develop your strengths?

> **Step 3: Align.** As you develop your strengths, also do your best to align your life with them. Maybe that means teaching or playing a music gig one night a week. Maybe it means exploring a new job that allows you to use your problem-solving or relationship-building skills. The more you are aligned with your strengths, the more you will be in flow with the harmony of life, which reduces stress and anxiety. List some possible ideas for aligning your life with your strengths.

Step 4: Invest. Exploring and harnessing your strengths, talents, and gifts means investing in yourself. While this can involve a financial investment, like hiring a coach or paying for classes, it also means investing time in building a supportive community and finding like-minded individuals. It could also mean investing in the tools, programs, and information you need to take your strengths to the next level. Usually it's a combination of all these things. What are some different ways you can invest in yourself and your strengths?

Step 5: Master. As your journey unfolds, you will develop an intimate relationship with your strengths and gifts, and you will eventually move into the zone of mastery. Dedication and deliberate practice of your craft is an essential part of your daily and weekly routines. A deep sense of fulfillment will emerge as your strengths become an extension of you rather than something you do. Mastery involves the transformation from doing the thing to being the thing. Your gifts merge into your beingness, allowing you to become one with them. Imagine achieving mastery in one or more areas: How different would your life look? How would it feel? What would you be doing?

Step 6: Adapt. Life is not linear. It's a series of ups and downs and unexpected turns. Sometimes we fall off course. The goal is to adapt so that your mastered skills and gifts, your sense of joy and purpose, don't lose their priority in your life. Much like a palm tree remains a palm tree through sunny days and category five hurricanes — allow your strengths to become the palm tree so they can withstand and adapt to life's various conditions. What are some ways you could adapt to keep your strengths at the forefront when life throws you curveballs?

Step 7: Create. You are a creator who is meant to create. Whether you are creating the work, experiences, art, your family — you are always creating. To turn your strengths into superpowers, you need to create experiences where you share your master-level strengths. Maybe you become a monthly contributor to a publication, create and sell art, start a podcast, improve or make new policies, or invent things and apply for patents. Whatever it is — create it and share it. How can you make room in your life to create more of what you love using your strengths? What are some ideas that pop up on how you can share your creative energy with the world?

Step 8: Evolve. As you create more experiences that are inclusive of your strengths, gifts, and talents, and as you share them with other people — you and your strengths will evolve. Go with the flow; stay curious about where they can lead and what can unfold. The truth is, working in the realm of your strengths puts you in a space of cocreation with the Universe, and infinite possibilities are possible. Keep learning, keep growing, keep experimenting. As your work evolves, so will you and your life. Imagine in the future that you have evolved into the person you were born to be in full expression of your strengths, gifts, and talents: What does it look like? What are you doing? How does it feel?

Reflecting on these eight steps in a journal will help you gain a deeper understanding and appreciation of your unique strengths. It also provides a structured path to actively harness and amplify these beautiful gifts, turning them into powerful assets in the unfolding of your infinite potential.

Superpowers Aren't Special, They're Essential

Everyone has gifts, talents, and strengths, and everyone can turn theirs into superpowers. When gifts, talents, and strengths are developed and allowed to shine, they aid in our journey of self-actualization. Turning them into superpowers helps us return to radiance. They are part of our soul's essence, just like our breath.

For example, my dad was a civil engineer, and one of his strengths was his high intellect and ability to solve problems. He fine-tuned those strengths as he progressed in his career. One of his gifts was being an avid storyteller, which expressed itself in his work, his music, and his interactions with others. His natural-born talent was playing the guitar at a high-caliber level. All three elements were part of his radiance.

For my dad, his soul needed him to play guitar to feel alive. Playing guitar was part of his cosmic DNA. It was a bridge between the seen and unseen worlds. It was his connection to the Universe, himself, and others. His guitar was the gateway for his strengths and gifts to shine brightly and unapologetically. We are all born with a unique combination of strengths, gifts, and talents that we can turn into superpowers. When we lean into them, not only can we create awe-inspiring results, we connect to passion and we feel fulfilled.

Imagine feeling less anxious, less stressed, and more confident and clear. That's what's in store when you turn your strengths into superpowers. Most of us know what lights us up, even if we don't know why. We know what we are good at. This is your invitation to claim your inherent gifts from the cosmos and fold them into your daily life.

Don't shy away from exploring what your strengths, talents, and gifts are, for they are the key to unlocking possibilities and unleashing your infinite potential.

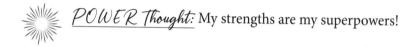

Grab Your Gemstone: Align your life and career with your strengths, talents, and gifts to the best of your ability, and invest in developing these assets. By doing so, you can transform them into superpowers, leading to a state of flow, reduced stress, and a deeper connection with your higher self and the Universe.

POWER Thought: My strengths are my superpowers!

POWER Up Your Practice 9: Discover Your Superpowers

Sometimes it's hard to pinpoint our own good qualities. They can feel so natural we might not recognize them or might dismiss them as common. In this exercise, choose at least three strengths, three gifts, and three talents that stand out as truth for you. Then each day, look for opportunities to develop these qualities and turn them into superpowers.

Strengths
- Leadership: The ability to guide and inspire others
- Empathy: Understanding and sharing the feelings of others
- Resilience: The capacity to recover quickly from difficulties
- Adaptability: Being able to adjust to new conditions
- Communication: Effective exchange of information
- Problem-solving: Finding solutions to complex issues
- Creativity: The use of imagination or original ideas
- Critical thinking: Analyzing facts to form a judgment
- Teamwork: Working effectively and harmoniously with others
- Time management: Efficiently managing one's time

Gifts
- Intuition: A deep instinctive knowing or understanding without rational explanation

- Compassion: Deep sympathy and sorrow for another stricken by misfortune, accompanied by a strong desire to alleviate the suffering
- Generosity: The willingness to give more of something than is strictly necessary or expected
- Wisdom: The quality of having experience, knowledge, and good judgment
- Inspiration: The ability to mentally stimulate others to do or feel something, especially to do something creative
- Healing: The capacity to help mend physical, emotional, or spiritual wounds in others
- Teaching: The natural ability to impart knowledge or skills effectively
- Peacemaking: The talent for resolving conflict or bringing about peaceful resolutions
- Joyfulness: A natural tendency to spread happiness and joy to others
- Hospitality: The friendly and generous reception and entertainment of guests, visitors, or strangers

Talents
- Artistic ability: Skills in areas such as painting, drawing, or sculpture
- Musicality: Natural skill or appreciation for music; playing instruments or singing
- Athleticism: Physical prowess and ability in sports or physical activities
- Numerical aptitude: Exceptional ability with numbers and math
- Linguistic talent: A natural affinity for languages and ease of learning them
- Photographic memory: The ability to remember information or visual images in great detail
- Spatial awareness: An innate understanding of space and dimensions

- Innate curiosity: A natural drive to learn, explore, and understand
- Mechanical skill: An inherent understanding of mechanical or technical principles
- Storytelling: The natural ability to tell compelling stories

Recognizing and nurturing these strengths, talents, and gifts can lead to personal fulfillment and success in various aspects of life, including relationships, careers, and personal growth.

CHAPTER TEN

Make Your Moves

$\mathcal{O}$ wning your opportunities helps to strengthen your connection to your radiance. And once you have learned how to change your meaning (to change your life), align with your values, calm self-doubt, and turn your strengths into superpowers, you are ready to take control of the trajectory of your outcomes by making your moves.

If you ever wanted to predict your future, you can look at three things: your routines, habits, and actions. The moment you take a good look at what's going on in each of these buckets, you can see whether they are empowering or disempowering you.

This chapter is meant to help you create a healthy relationship with your habits, actions, and routines to make sure they are serving you and supporting you to unleash that beautiful potential of yours. When you make your moves count, you are saying yes to life, and life says yes to you.

Routines for the Win

Routines provide structure and help us thrive, but they can also keep us stuck and stagnant depending on the quality of our routines. Take a quick minute to reflect on your routines. What do you do on a regular basis? Are your routines propelling you forward or are they holding you back?

Focus your energy on creating a routine that sets you up for success. Returning to radiance is an energy game. Your routines are either going to motivate you and keep you going or they are going to drain you and keep you stuck in the status quo. You are not here to play small. You are here to unleash your potential and enjoy the life you create. It's not so much about what you can achieve by creating awesome routines; it is more about the quality of life that you enjoy.

One of my clients, Fred, had a really terrible morning routine. Every morning, he rolled out of bed after hitting the snooze button at least three times, hopped in the shower, grabbed some mini-muffins as he flew out the door so he wasn't late for work, and took his first work call from the car. His morning looked like this for years. This ended up being the source of his troubles. By the time I started working with him and his organization, he felt successful. His accomplishments and awards certainly demonstrated that he was. Yet behind-the-scenes this sales leader was highly unsatisfied, and this is a common theme among those who have worked hard their entire careers yet wonder what all the hard work is even for. Can you relate?

Deep satisfaction is a spiritual game, and we have to ignite our soul to really feel it. Fred, like many others, was definitely disconnected from purpose and passion and wanted these back in his life. We started small with his morning routine, which was stressing out his nervous system by not giving it anything nourishing. Fred told me that something he used to do, which he loved, was going for long-distance bike rides. Bingo! Here was something we could leverage to create a more-supportive morning routine for him.

Fred admitted that his morning routines left no space for him to just be Fred. He agreed to waking up forty-five minutes earlier to go on a bike ride for twenty minutes or more. This would help generate more healthy hormones, help regulate his mood, and get him moving and outside in the elements before starting work. Fred agreed to one rule: No talking on the cell phone.

Changing one routine provided extraordinary results for Fred.

By creating a more supportive and healthy start to his morning, Fred began to enjoy life again, and ultimately his feelings of satisfaction increased. This impacted the way he perceived life as well. He was able to see how life supported him, which allowed him to make more decisions that helped him thrive.

Review your routines to see if they are serving you or sabotaging you. Especially as you start to use your strengths as superpowers, your routines need to support you. Here are some questions to ask. If you wish, explore your answers in a journal.

- What time do you wake up? How many times do you hit the snooze button? What's the first thing you do? Do you spend any time outside? Are you physically active? If so, what does that look like?
- Do you journal, creative-write, or meditate? If so, what activities do you do to start your day?
- Do you drink coffee or tea? Do you prepare your food for the day?
- Do you ease into your morning or rush into it with tight timelines?
- What do your midday routines look like?
- Do you break for lunch? If so, what do you typically eat for lunch?
- Do you rejuvenate at all during the day? Perhaps with a walk or by reading a book? If so, what do you do?
- What do you do after work?
- Do you have time connecting with loved ones? Are you always on your phone?
- Do you have your meals prepped and planned or do you eat takeout most often?
- What qualities of your evening routine do you like and dislike?
- Are you typically satisfied with your day?
- What are your end-of-day routines?

What stands out the most as you consider these questions? Identify one or two tweaks that would make your routines more satisfying and fulfilling. Routines for the win is about micro changes and not massive changes. Small actions are easier and can lead to big outcomes, while big actions can bog down and lead to no change. I know this might sound counterintuitive but it's true. The most satisfied people make one move at a time — and that is all you need to do for now. Make one move.

Brain Hacking with Habit Stacking

Fred's story didn't end there. At first, Fred couldn't see how he would ever be able to ride his bike for more than twenty minutes every morning. He really believed that twenty minutes was the max, and he listed sixteen reasons why. However, about a month after Fred began biking for twenty minutes, he increased his ride to an hour every morning, plus he started running and replaced a sugary breakfast with a protein shake paired with fresh fruit. This is a perfect illustration of "habit stacking," one of my favorite tools for hacking the brain for our own good.

Habit stacking is a productivity technique that helps you make your moves more successfully and with less overwhelm. If I had asked Fred to start training for a triathlon (which he eventually did) and to change his diet, he probably would have laughed in my face. He'd have given me fifty reasons why he couldn't do it. Instead, we started small and attached new good habits to existing ones. By doing this, you get to leverage the power of your routines to instill positive behaviors, feel more satisfied, and achieve your goals. Since habits are formed through repetition and consistency, piggybacking new habits a little bit at a time ensures that they become sustainable and integrate seamlessly into your routines.

For example, if your goal is to read more books, you could stack the habit of reading onto an existing habit of drinking coffee in the morning. Every time you make your morning coffee, you commit to reading for ten minutes before starting your day. Over time, this simple habit stack becomes ingrained in your routines, allowing you to consistently engage in reading without feeling overwhelmed or stressed about finding time for it.

When we habit stack, we hack our brain and convince it we are only making one small change. Our brain doesn't perceive small changes as a threat, so it allows us to do them without inspiring a whole bunch of self-questioning and resistance.

Instead of making massive changes, you can make your moves one awesome new habit at a time, stacked on top of previous ones. Eventually, your routines will consistent of things that ignite your soul and enhance your vitality.

Can you think of a time where you accidentally or purposefully habit stacked? What was the outcome? Are there any habits you would like to change? If so, list how you could habit stack and the order you would start. Then do it.

Three, Two, One, Action

Taking action is essential to making your dreams and desires come to fruition. First, action transforms ideas and aspirations into tangible reality. Without action, dreams have a hard time manifesting into reality. Action also generates momentum and progress toward goals, propelling us forward and helping us achieve milestones. Each step taken brings us closer to our aspirations, building confidence and motivation along the way.

Taking action helps us learn and grow by providing valuable feedback and insights. Through action, we gain firsthand experience, learn from mistakes, and refine our approaches, increasing our chances of success. Action builds character and amplifies qualities like commitment and determination, signaling to ourselves and others that the pursuit of our goals and dreams is possible. It shows a willingness to overcome obstacles, persevere through challenges, and seize opportunities, regardless of setbacks.

Ultimately, taking action is the catalyst that transforms dreams into reality, empowering us to create the life we've envisioned for ourselves.

The biggest tip for incorporating action into your daily make-your-moves practice is to just do it — three, two, one, action! Once you take the first step and just do it, you are no longer ruminating on when, why, and how. You are doing. It is in the doing that you become self-reliant, and you begin to understand that you are capable and adaptable. Taking action is one of life's biggest teachers because we learn when we fail, and we learn when we succeed. Learning is how we grow and discover who we are and who we are meant to be. Learning lights our path toward self-actualization and unleashes our potential. The next time you are considering making a move and not sure if it's worth it, ask yourself this: If I take action, will I learn something regardless of failure or success? If the answer is yes, then three, two, one, action yourself into it.

Positive Feedback Loop

Positive feedback loops are produced by our brain and body chemistry and are a mechanism by which we can create more favorable outcomes, since positive behaviors and actions are reinforced. Positive feedback loops play a crucial role in promoting consistency, motivation, and forward progress in the direction of our dreams and goals.

For example, let's say your goal is to write a book, and you decide to incorporate thirty minutes of writing in your morning routine. Initially, you may find it hard to motivate yourself to write when you have other things to do. However, each time you sit down and write, you experience immediate benefits, such as increased energy, improved mood, and a sense of accomplishment. These positive outcomes serve as rewards for your behavior, reinforcing the habit of writing. As you continue your daily writes and reap those rewards, the positive feedback loop strengthens, making it more likely that you will stick to your writing practice long-term.

Developing healthy routines, employing habit stacking techniques, and taking action generate a positive result in your mind, body, and soul. You begin to transform from the inside out. On the outside, it might look as though you only made one or two changes. Yet on the inside, far more is going on. Your soul is glowing up.

Here are seven benefits to making your moves count with supportive and regenerative routines, habits, and actions:

1. Enhanced motivation: Achieving a single habit instills a sense of fulfillment and encouragement. This positivity serves as fuel to propel you toward tackling subsequent habits, establishing a continuous loop of motivation and action.

2. Commitment to consistency: By adhering consistently to your routine and integrating habits, you reinforce a pattern of behavior. Each completed habit reinforces this pattern, bolstering your commitment to maintaining your routine over time.

3. Optimized efficiency: Habit stacking allows you to capitalize on existing habits as triggers for new ones. By intertwining fresh behaviors with established routines, you streamline your daily regimen and maximize your time management.

4. Continuous growth: Over time, habit stacking facilitates the accumulation of small victories and gradual enhancements. As you introduce new habits and build upon existing ones, you foster personal development across various aspects of your life.

5. Heightened confidence: Each successful completion of a habit cultivates a sense of self-assurance and efficacy.

This confidence reaffirms your belief in your capacity to pursue your goals and habits, fortifying your dedication to positive transformation.

6. Less decision fatigue: Automating certain behaviors through habit stacking diminishes the need for repetitive decision-making throughout the day. This liberation conserves mental energy and willpower, allowing for enhanced cognitive function and productivity.

7. Increased well-being: Engaging in healthy habits and routines yields a host of benefits for your overall wellness. From physical advantages like enhanced fitness and improved sleep to mental perks such as stress reduction and heightened resilience, establishing a positive feedback loop through habit stacking can contribute to a more joyful, healthier life.

Fostering a positive feedback loop via healthy routines, habit stacking, and taking action serves to reinforce good behaviors, amplify motivation and consistency, nurture personal growth, and ultimately elevate the quality of life. How awesome is that?

By harnessing the potency of your routines, habits, and actions, you can create positive change, feel fabulous, and own your future opportunities. So, fierce one, go out into the world and make your moves!

Grab Your Gemstone: Owning your opportunities is essential for strengthening your connection to your radiance and unleashing your potential. Embracing supportive routines, habit stacking, and taking action can lead to enhanced motivation, commitment, efficiency, growth, confidence, decision-making, and overall well-being, ultimately empowering you to own your opportunities and make your moves with confidence and purpose.

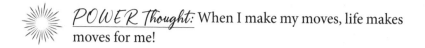 _POWER Thought:_ When I make my moves, life makes moves for me!

POWER Up Your Practice 10: Make New Moves

This exercise will help you summarize what you want your life to look like and what is important to you so you can prioritize it into your life by making new moves.

Grab your journal or your favorite way to write. Let's get started:

- Identify priorities: Determine what matters most to you and what you want to accomplish. Identify tasks, habits, and activities that align with your values, goals, and well-being. Write down the ones that matter to you the most.

- Establish a schedule: Set specific times for each activity within your routine, taking into account your natural rhythms and energy levels. Allocate more time to high-priority tasks and activities that require focus or creativity. What can you add into your routine and when?

- Start small: If you're new to routines or making significant changes, start with a simple, manageable structure. Focus on incorporating a few key habits or activities at a time and gradually building upon them. What are one or two new habits that you can add to your routines that feel the most important?

- Be flexible: Embrace flexibility and view deviations as opportunities to learn and grow. What are some ways in which you will give yourself grace and restart if you fall off your schedule?

- Optimize your environment: Create an environment that minimizes distractions and supports your routines, habits, and new actions. Set up dedicated spaces for specific activities, remove clutter, and eliminate potential obstacles to staying on track. How can you optimize your environment?

- Prioritize self-care: Make self-care a nonnegotiable part of your routines. Schedule time for activities that recharge and nourish you, such as exercise, meditation, hobbies, and spending time with loved ones. What self-care practices are you committed to having as part of your daily or weekly routines?
- Reflect and adjust: Regularly evaluate your routines to assess their effectiveness and identify areas for improvement. Reflect on what's working well and what could be modified or eliminated. Adjust your routines as needed to better align with your evolving needs and priorities.
- Stay consistent: Consistency is key to the success of your routines. Commit to following your routines consistently, even on days when motivation is low or obstacles arise. Over time, consistency strengthens habits and creates a positive feedback loop that allows life to support you as you pursue your goals and dreams.

By creating supportive routines tailored to your needs and priorities, you can cultivate habits that enhance your well-being, productivity, and overall quality of life.

PART THREE

WAKEN YOUR
Worthiness

The important thing to know about worthiness is
that it doesn't have prerequisites.

— Brené Brown

CHAPTER ELEVEN

Activate Your Personal Power

*Y*ou are born worthy of it all — health, wealth, happiness, and the full manifestation of your potential. All of this is written in the cosmos for you to achieve here in this lifetime. The spirit of your ancestors got you here, and the spirit of the great Universe will carry you forward. This is what I want you to know: Activating your personal power will help you achieve all that you were born to be and more.

Personal power is inner power that is yours alone, and it is linked directly to your worthiness. You can think of your personal power as the water in the hose, and the hose as the medium that either lets your personal power flow or gets a kink and limits it. The activation process mirrors turning the faucet on and increasing the pressure, or you can decrease the pressure and turn it off. When you waken your worthiness — the third part of the POWER Method — your pressure is strong, your hose is straight, and your power is flowing. When your worthiness is compromised, your pressure is weak, there are kinks in the hose, and your power is either off or barely flowing.

It's important to understand the link between your personal power and your worthiness because oftentimes your inner power leaks out through holes in the hose, which impacts your worthiness and prevents you from shining in your radiance. These holes can be caused by letting someone else make your decisions, holding yourself back from living your truth, or molding yourself to someone else's expectations. That is why part one of the POWER

Method is about protecting your potential, and part two is about owning your opportunities — you can think of these two parts as hole prevention.

When your worthiness is intentionally tended to every day, it allows you to claim what is inherently yours — health, wealth, happiness, and fulfillment — with more grace and ease.

ROAR!

When was the last time you roared like a lion? Never? Maybe when you were a kid?

But did you know that roaring activates your personal power? Your personal power lies dormant until activated. Similar to turning on the faucet to fill the hose, you want to turn on or activate your personal power every day to ensure that you can chase your dreams and claim your desires with unwavering assurance. Literally roaring out loud is one fun and surefire way to waken your worthiness.

Why is it important to awaken your inner power? Here are six primary benefits to roaring and activating your inner power.

1. Awakened intuition and instincts: In today's world, with bills, work, and responsibilities, people are more disconnected from themselves than they have ever been. This means they are disconnected from their power, which in turn means they are disconnected from their intuition and instincts, which is why so many people feel indecisive and seek outside themselves for answers. Roaring connects you to the innate knowing inside.

2. Embraced authenticity: Social pressure and constraints bend and contort most people away from their authentic core. Our need for belonging is high, so it's easy for most people to abandon the truth of who they are for acceptance and validation from others. You were born to be different

and your uniqueness makes up your radiance and is exactly what the world needs. So roar away to get real.

3. Harnessed inner strength: Stress weakens our inner strength. Then we get stuck there. Roaring releases stress and taps into our inner reservoir of strength, courage, and resilience. This inner power enables us to overcome challenges, face adversity, and turn our setbacks into success with unwavering determination.

4. Connection with nature: Suburban life for most working professionals can disconnect them from nature and Universal presence. Magic and wonder seem to fade in the distance. Roaring connects us back to our natural self. It elicits feelings of creativity and connectedness to the environment and the world. It encourages us to get out into the world and reconnect with nature, boosting our sense of wholeness and overall well-being.

5. Supercharged vitality: Disease is on the rise and vitality is on the decline. These are clear signs that, as a society, we are far away from our radiance and much closer to our UN-potential. Roaring helps to activate our personal power, which in turn supercharges our vitality. This allows us to shine in the glory of our radiance, igniting passion and unleashing potential along the way.

6. Enhanced personal leadership: With disconnection from ourselves and our cosmic connection being a widespread problem, this translates to a large majority of folks — unintentionally — stepping out of their personal power. This makes it harder for us to lead others, let alone ourselves. Our inner power is decisive and unquestioning. Roaring helps connect to the leader within and enhances our overall leadership skills.

For centuries, the lion has stood as a symbol of strength and power, transcending boundaries of religion and culture. Its regal presence and commanding stature embody notions of royalty and nobility, epitomizing qualities of majesty, leadership, and power. Consider ancient Egypt, where lions were often depicted in art and myth as symbolic emblems of kingship, which the pharaohs embraced.

In the realms of folklore and mythology, lions are often fearless and noble beings, embodiments of courage and valor that inspire awe in the face of adversity. The resounding roar of the lion symbolizes an indomitable spirit, igniting the flames of strength and fortitude within. Their roar serves as a potent reminder of our own inner power, particularly in moments of stagnation and helplessness.

The lion also represents spiritual significance across diverse faiths. In Christianity, it embodies Christ's authority and might as well as the virtues of courage and righteousness. Similarly, in Hinduism, the lion is a divine symbol, linked to deities, and revered for sovereignty and divine protection.

In essence, the lion and its roar have been regarded throughout history as embodiments of the virtues of strength, courage, and spirituality, which are essential qualities in wakening and claiming our worthiness. Its symbolic resonance serves as a timeless reminder of our innate potential and resilience, urging us to embrace our own inner power and move forward with unwavering confidence and grace as we return to radiance.

So the next time that you are alone in your home or your car — ROAR! Your personal power is waiting to be activated.

Wakening Your Worthiness

What is worthiness exactly? Worthiness as it relates to our inherent worth is the concept that every individual is valuable and deserving of love, respect, and kindness, regardless of circumstances, actions, or life choices. It's not something that is earned through achievements, status, or the approval of others. Within your radiance is the manifestation of the fullness of your gifts and your potential. There is already an expression of the true you, self-actualized, seeded in you at birth. Your job is to tend to and nurture it.

My goal isn't to convince you that you are worthy — because you already are. I want to give you tools to awaken and activate your worthiness. Consciously turning on your power every day just like turning on the faucet gives you the fortitude necessary to have the courage and strength to go after and claim what is already yours.

This book is filled with techniques that can help you activate your power, in addition to roaring. Consider the list below and decide which resonate with you the most. Then flag the exercises related to them as you read and try to incorporate them into your daily practice, so you activate your inner power every day.

- Breathwork: Kundalini breathing techniques help increase vitality, activate inner power, and circulate energy throughout the body. See chapter 16 for more on Kundalini yoga, and see chapter 18 for breathing techniques, as well as this chapter's practice, "Breath of Fire with Root Lock."
- Movement and postures: Yoga postures, stomping around, and shamanic dance movements all help release physical tension, open energetic channels, and connect with the primal rhythms of the body. These movements activate the flow of personal power, allowing it to move freely through the body. For more, see chapter 16.
- Mantras and chanting: Chanting sacred sounds, mantras, and affirmations are powerful ways to activate this energy and align with higher consciousness. This helps to awaken our dormant power and connect with the vibration of the Universe. Chapter 19 discusses mantras.
- Meditation and visualization: Guided meditations that

involve music and visualization techniques assist in accessing deeper states of consciousness and help activate personal power. Through guided imagery and focused intention, we become one with our inner wisdom and our warrior spirit. See chapter 20 for an overview of meditation.

- Time outside: Spending time in natural environments, communing with plants, animals, and the elements, helps align with the primal rhythms of the Earth. Standing barefoot in the grass or allowing the sun to hit your face for just a few minutes a day can serve as a mood booster as well as an energy enhancer that activates your inner power.

By integrating these practices into your everyday life, you can awaken your personal power, deepen your connection with the natural world, and access the limitless potential that resides within you. Choose the ones that feel the best and most comfortable for you and start there. There is no limit to the techniques you can try. This energy is wise and ancient — and it's sitting and waiting to be activated to serve you.

Grab Your Gemstone: Your personal power shines with the timeless wisdom of thousands of years of ancestry and the boundless energy of the Universe. This inner power fuels your resilience, vitality, and authenticity, empowering you to awaken your worthiness and embrace your true potential.

POWER Thought: My inner power unlocks my unstoppable spirit!

POWER Up Your Practice 11: Breath of Fire with Root Lock

Everyone breathes. Not everyone breathes with intention. Our breath is the most valuable part of our being. The first thing we do as we enter the world is inhale and the last thing we do as we exit is exhale. Your breath can be both instinctual and intentional.

In Kundalini yoga, our primal power is known as our kundalini. It is our life-force energy. When this dormant energy, which rests at the base of our spine, is activated, it awakens and moves up through us as if it were traveling up our spine until it reaches the crown of our head. At this point, our life-force energy merges with that of Infinite Intelligence and comes back into our being with heightened awareness and insight. This ultimately strengthens our intuition and instincts.

Learning how to use your breath to activate your primal power is a game changer that improves confidence, clarity, and conviction. You will break through indecision, optimize your health, and greet life with energy and enthusiasm, which will create new opportunities. Practiced over time, the "Breath of Fire" technique, and the other Kundalini breathwork practices in this book, can lead to even more growth, including spiritual enlightenment, expanded consciousness, and profound personal transformation.

This exercise combines two techniques from Kundalini yoga — Breath of Fire and Root Lock. Together, these activate your primal power. Remember, you can download the complimentary Return to Radiance Personal Transformation Guide, which contains all the POWER Up Your Practice exercises, at Resources.ReturnToRadiance Book.com.

Breath of Fire

Breath of Fire is a powerful breathing technique used in Kundalini yoga to increase energy, build internal heat, and purify the body.

Remember to practice mindfully; listen to your body's signals and adjust the pace and intensity as needed. With regular practice, Breath of Fire can help increase vitality, improve focus and concentration, and promote overall well-being by activating your inner power and wakening your worthiness.

Here's a step-by-step guide:

- Sit comfortably on the floor, such as cross-legged (called easy pose) or on a chair with your feet flat on the floor. Sit with your spine straight and shoulders relaxed, with your chin parallel to the ground. Close your eyes.
- Breath of Fire involves rapid and rhythmic breathing through the nostrils while engaging the muscles of the diaphragm and abdomen. Practice once or twice by taking a few deep breaths to connect with your breath and activate your abdominal muscles. Inhale fully through your nose and exhale forcefully and quickly out through your nose, as if trying to blow out a candle.
- Once your abdominals are engaged, place one hand on your diaphragm. Inhale slowly and deeply through the nose and feel your abdomen expand, pushing out. Using a slow controlled exhale, let all the air out and notice your abdomen pulling in toward your spine. Do this a few times.
- When you are ready to begin, start inhaling and exhaling through your nose, contracting your abdominal muscles to exhale sharply while completely emptying the air from your lungs. Maintain a comfortable pace and follow a steady one-two rhythm (one for inhale, two for exhale) that mimics a puppy panting. Allow your inhalations to occur naturally after each exhale, with no pause between breaths. If you wish, gradually increase your pace as you become more accustomed to the practice.
- Practice the Breath of Fire for a set duration. The first time, this might be as short as one minute. As you become more

comfortable with the technique, gradually increase the duration to three minutes.

- Once the planned duration is over, complete the practice by taking a deep inhale through your nose, filling your lungs with air, and exhaling slowly and completely through your mouth. Allow your breathing to return to normal as you notice any sensations or changes in your body and breath.

Root Lock

Once you've finished Breath of Fire, apply Root Lock:

- Take another deep inhale through the nose and suspend your breath. As you hold your breath, pull up on your sex organs and anus, and contract your lower region up and in. You should feel slight pressure as you apply tension to the lower region. Envision your dormant primal power activating at the base of your spine. Then imagine this power traveling up your spine and leaving out through the crown of your scalp and merging with Infinite Intelligence.
- When your visualization is done, exhale powerfully through the nose and return to slow deep breathing. Finally, open your eyes and write down any experiences or feelings that came up for you.

CHAPTER TWELVE

The Seeds of Faith

*H*ave you ever seriously wondered whether gravity is going to stop working and you will float off into the cosmos? Of course not. At no time has Earth's gravity ever not done its job, and so we live reassured that we won't float away.

This is an example of faith in action. Faith can be something that operates on autopilot — like faith in gravity — and it can also be something we actively cultivate. Unlike gravity, faith in our inherent worthiness is often something that needs to be cultivated, since we can doubt whether we are truly deserving of health, wealth, happiness, and fulfillment. This doubt gets in the way of experiencing these things.

This chapter explores how faith can be used as a tool to waken your worthiness. In the context of returning to radiance, I consider faith to be the ability and the confidence to trust in both yourself and Infinite Intelligence.

Faith in yourself and the Universe has the power to restore hope when all feels lost. It has the power to transform the impossible into the possible, and it can heal when you need it most. Above all, faith keeps you connected to your higher self, others, and Infinite Intelligence.

Grandma's Mustard Seed

"Becca Ann, hold out your hand," said Grandma West. I trusted my grandma with all of myself. I did as Grandma asked and held out my hand. I knew she was going to give me something, and I was hoping for one of her strawberry candies. Instead, Grandma West put a tiny seed in my hand.

I looked up at her with confusion and said, "Grandma, what is this?" My grandma replied, "It's a mustard seed. I want to teach you about faith. All you need is faith the size of this mustard seed and God's got the rest." Grandma's conviction told me she was sharing something important. With curiosity, I asked, "Like Pinocchio did when he wished upon a star?" She replied, "Well, I never really thought about it that way but yes. Faith is more than just wishing upon a star, though. Becca Ann, you also need to have faith in yourself."

I was only five. I didn't understand religion or that my grandma was teaching me something from the Bible. What I understood was that my grandma was teaching me something about life. Grandma's mustard seed story taught me two valuable lessons that have been reinforced through the years. Lesson one: I was worthy of believing and having faith in myself. With faith in myself and my abilities, I am willing to take more intentional risks because I have faith that I can adapt and figure things out as I go. Lesson two: Faith is a tool I can use to lighten my load. Over the years, as I have embarked on new journeys or received life-altering information or have had more on my plate than I can handle, I know I can rely on the Universe to support me. All I need is just a seed-sized amount of faith and the belief that Infinite Intelligence can handle the rest.

Let's explore Grandma's mustard seed lessons further.

Lesson One: Faith in Yourself

Having faith in yourself means trusting in your abilities, decisions, and worth, even in the face of uncertainty or adversity. It involves believing in your capacity to navigate challenges, achieve your goals, and handle life's ups and downs effectively.

This kind of faith encompasses a deep-seated confidence that you are capable of growth, learning, and making meaningful contributions.

Faith in yourself also implies a resilience that allows you to bounce back from setbacks and persist despite failures or criticisms. It encourages a positive outlook on personal potential and capabilities, fostering a proactive attitude toward life's opportunities. Essentially, having faith in yourself is about embracing your own strengths and capabilities while acknowledging and working on your areas of opportunity without judgment or harsh self-criticism. This self-belief acts as a foundation for not only personal success and happiness but also for how you interact with and influence the world around you.

Strengthening your faith in yourself and affirming your worthiness can be significantly enhanced by reflecting on certain empowering questions. Here are five thoughtful questions you can ask yourself to deepen your self-belief and reinforce your sense of inherent worth:

FIVE QUESTIONS TO STRENGTHEN FAITH AND WORTHINESS

1. What are my strengths and how have they helped me in the past?
    - Reflect on your abilities and past successes. Recognizing how your unique qualities have positively impacted your life can boost your confidence and faith in your capabilities.

2. What challenges have I overcome, and what did they teach me about my resilience and resourcefulness?
    - Considering the difficulties you've faced and how you've surmounted them can highlight your resilience, reinforcing your belief and faith in your ability to handle future challenges.

3.   In what ways can I contribute positively to the lives of others?

   o   Thinking about how you can or have made a difference in others' lives can solidify your sense of purpose and worthiness.

4.   How do I support and treat myself during tough times?

   o   Assessing how you care for yourself during difficult periods can improve your self-compassion and reinforce your worthiness of self-care and love.

5.   What would I do if I fully believed in my abilities and worth?

   o   Imagining the possibilities can open up new pathways for action that are grounded in confidence and self-assurance.

Lesson Two: Faith in the Universe to Support You

Having faith in the Universe to support you, in relation to your inherent worth, involves trusting that the Universe is fundamentally benevolent and that it is working in ways that align with your best interests. This belief is rooted in the idea that there is a positive purpose behind the events and experiences in your life, even if they might not immediately seem beneficial.

Here's what having faith in the Universe typically encompasses:

• Alignment with life's purpose: Believing that Infinite Intelligence supports you is often linked to the idea that everyone has a purpose or a role to play in life. Trusting in this support means feeling that the Universe will guide you toward experiences that align with this purpose, helping you to grow, learn, and contribute in ways that fulfill your inherent potential.

- Positive outcomes from challenges: Faith in the Universe involves seeing challenges not as mere obstacles but as opportunities designed for personal growth and evolution. It's the belief that even in difficulty, there is a supportive element guiding you toward a greater understanding and strengthening of your own worth.
- Synchronicity and timing: This faith can manifest as trust in the timing of your life's events. It's an acceptance that things happen not always when you want them to, but when they need to for the optimal outcome. There is an underlying assurance that the Universe's timing is perfect in the context of your life's journey.
- Deserving good things: Faith in the Universe's support is also tied to a belief in your own worthiness to receive good things. It negates the notion that you must earn love, success, and happiness, reinforcing instead that these are things you deserve simply by virtue of being yourself.
- Letting go of control: Having faith in the Universe involves a willingness to surrender control. Rather than trying to force life to unfold in specific ways, it's about releasing the reins and allowing life to flow naturally, trusting that this process will guide you to where you need to be.
- Inner peace: Ultimately, this type of faith contributes to a profound sense of peace and contentment. Knowing that Infinite Intelligence is looking out for you can reduce anxiety and fear about the future, enabling a more joyful and present engagement with life.

What Makes Faith an Asset

Faith is free, yet what it delivers is priceless, especially when you have faith in yourself and the ability of the Universe to support you. If you aren't used to trusting yourself, having faith in yourself might feel weird. That's why waking your worthiness starts by activating your inner power (chapter 11). When your power is activated, your intuition and instincts are heightened, putting you in a better position to trust yourself.

One thing to keep in mind about faith: It doesn't care what you look like or what you do for a living — it only cares about supporting your outcomes in your highest and greatest good. Imagine having full faith in yourself and truly believing you can do the things you want to do — that you are not only capable but will be successful in your pursuits. Take a moment to visualize this. See one of your desires fully manifested in your imagination. Within you is the ability to bring this to reality. Faith plus intentional action makes room for the impossible to become possible.

Another thing that makes faith an asset is that it creates a positive feedback loop of self-trust. It can strengthen your internal relationship with your inner wisdom and capabilities. When we don't trust ourselves, we look outside ourselves for answers. When we constantly search outside ourselves, the disconnection between ourselves, our soul, and the world becomes greater.

When you have faith in yourself, you seek within for wisdom. When you trust yourself, you trust the Universe because you are listening to the whispers of your soul. As a result, you believe in yourself and Infinite Intelligence guiding you. This trust eventually converts into unwavering faith — and that, fierce one, is when your potential unleashes.

Trusting yourself can have numerous health and lifestyle benefits, too. It fosters a sense of self-assurance, resilience, and empowerment. Here are some key advantages to cultivating the seeds of faith in your life:

- Reduced stress and anxiety: Trusting yourself allows you to feel more confident in your decisions and abilities, reducing uncertainties and doubts that can contribute to stress and anxiety.
- Improved mental well-being: When you have faith in

yourself, you cultivate a positive self-image and inner strength, which enhances self-esteem and self-worth. This can lead to greater overall satisfaction with life and improved mental well-being.

- Alignment of choices and values: Trusting yourself enables you to make decisions more confidently and assertively. You become better at listening to your intuition and instincts, leading to more authentic and fulfilling choices that align with your values and goals.

- More resilience: Having faith in yourself means believing in your capacity to overcome challenges and setbacks. This resilience helps you bounce back more quickly from adversity and navigate life's ups and downs with more ease and grace.

- Increased independence: Trusting yourself fosters independence and self-reliance, as you become less dependent on external validation or approval. You feel more empowered to take ownership of your life and pursue your goals with autonomy and determination.

- Improved relationships: When you have faith in yourself, you're better able to establish healthy boundaries, communicate effectively, and assert your needs in relationships. This fosters deeper connections based on mutual respect and understanding.

- Better physical health: Trusting yourself can positively impact your physical health by reducing stress-related symptoms and promoting behaviors that support well-being, such as regular exercise, healthy eating, and restful sleep.

Overall, trusting yourself is foundational to leading a fulfilling and balanced life. It empowers you to navigate life's challenges with confidence, authenticity, and resilience. Ultimately, it contributes to your overall health and well-being as well as wakening your worthiness to express the fullness of your potential.

Flex Your Faith Muscles

If you are currently chasing bills, responsibilities, and work rather than hopes, dreams, and fulfillment, then this is a great opportunity to flex your faith muscles. In the absence of faith, we can become disconnected from our truth and our radiance. The truth is that we either live in faith or fear — so why not try faith?

What is it that you desire most? What do you daydream about? Answering these questions will identify where you need to activate your faith muscles. Just like working out by going to the gym, faith muscles only grow when we use them.

To build your faith muscles, follow these four steps:

Step 1: Believe in possibility. There are infinite possibilities that exist in the great big cosmos and these possibilities are available to you. Believe in your potential and the possibility for success. You can create a life that supports your deepest desires and achieve extraordinary results. Your first step is to believe in possibility. What would open up for you if you believed it were possible?

Step 2: Reinforce empowering thoughts. Your thoughts shape your beliefs, and your beliefs shape your perceptions. They influence your decisions and your actions. If you feel plagued by negative thoughts, become a thought ninja and karate chop negative thoughts as they pass through. Then reinforce empowering thoughts in their place. This will help strengthen your faith muscles. What would you do if you believed you could?

Step 3: Set stretch goals. Our brains love certainty and a plan. Let faith be the vehicle of certainty and a stretch goal be the plan. Write a goal that supports one of your desired outcomes. The goal should only be two to three steps ahead of where you are now. Once you successfully reach these goals, your trust and confidence in yourself will increase. What goals are obtainable with a little extra effort and focus?

Step 4: Radiate resilience. Fear hates action. Faith loves it. Every time you fall, dust yourself off and try again. You are learning, growing, and becoming more of who you are each time you face the unknown with optimism. Radiate resiliency from your unstoppable spirit. Step boldly into possibility and watch as the most magical and unexpected opportunities begin to unfold. If you knew you could not fail, how would your actions be different?

Grab Your Gemstone: Faith embodies the timeless wisdom of the Universe, empowering you to withstand challenges, expect miracles, and move forward with unwavering trust in yourself and the infinite potential of the cosmos.

POWER Thought: I trust myself and the Universe to lead me to beautiful outcomes!

POWER Up Your Practice 12: Trusting Self and the Universe Meditation

This guided meditation is meant to deepen your trust in yourself and the Universe. Trust is the cornerstone of personal growth and fulfillment, allowing you to navigate life's challenges with confidence and grace. Through this practice, you tap into your inner wisdom and connect with the limitless support of the Universe.

- Find a quiet and comfortable space where you can sit or lie down without distractions. Take a few moments to settle into your chosen position, allowing your body to relax and your mind to become still.

- Close your eyes and take several deep breaths, inhaling slowly through your nose and exhaling fully through your mouth. With each breath, feel yourself becoming more grounded and centered in the present moment.

- Bring your awareness to your heart center, the seat of your intuition and inner knowing. Visualize a warm, golden light glowing within your heart, radiating love, compassion, and trust.

- As you continue to breathe deeply, imagine this golden light expanding outward, enveloping your entire body in a cocoon of warmth and protection. Feel the reassuring presence of this light, reminding you that you are safe, supported, and guided at all times.

- With each inhale, affirm to yourself, *I trust myself completely.* Feel the truth of these words resonating within, strengthening your self-confidence and belief in your abilities. Do this three times.

- Now shift your focus to the Universe, the vast and infinite source of wisdom and abundance. Visualize a stream of shimmering light descending from the cosmos, flowing directly into your heart center.

- As this radiant light fills you, repeat the affirmation, *I trust in the Universe's plan for me.* Allow yourself to surrender to the divine flow of life, knowing that everything unfolds in perfect timing for your highest good. Do this three times.

- Take a few moments to bask in the sensation of trust and connection, allowing yourself to be fully present in the embrace of the Universe's love and guidance.

- When you feel ready, gently bring your awareness back to your physical surroundings. Wiggle your fingers and toes, stretch your body, and slowly open your eyes.

- Take a moment to reflect on your experience, noticing any shifts or insights that arise during the meditation. Trust that you can return to this place of inner peace and trust whenever you need to realign with yourself and the Universe.

If you practice this meditation regularly, you will strengthen your bond with yourself and the Universe, deepening your trust in the divine unfolding of your life's journey. Remember that trust is a lifelong practice, and each moment offers an opportunity to reaffirm your faith in yourself and the limitless possibilities of the Universe. Trust in the process, and let your inner light guide you confidently on your path to fulfillment and joy.

CHAPTER THIRTEEN

Bear-Hug Uncomfortable

*H*ave you ever started something new and felt so uncomfortable you thought you were going to get sick? Did you stop or did you keep going? Our nervous systems are wired to be skeptical of change, and our souls are wired for adventure. Depending on the day, either one could win. This is where we have to power up choices and keep going. That upset stomach is a sign that whatever we are about to embark on is both scary and exciting — and that's OK. Bear-hugging uncomfortable is about embracing change with excitement — like we would an old friend.

Change is never going to be comfortable. What's more uncomfortable? Staying the same. Gosh, if I could rewind time and tell my parents that settling for the life society prescribed them was the exact thing that would make them disconnect from their radiance, I would do so in a second. Returning to your radiance is not going to be comfortable, but it will be rewarding. You are reclaiming your worth and your personal power. That's not easy. It's not the path most walk. It's the path, however, that turns uncomfortable new beginnings into extraordinary realities — and that's why we want to tightly embrace change with a sense of wonder.

My parents could have chosen the path less traveled and lived a life full of fulfillment and passion like they once had. But that didn't feel like an option to them. The more uncomfortable path may have changed their schedules, income, and availability — for the better. Yet the fear of that leading to a bad outcome versus a good one was enough to prevent them from taking proactive steps toward positive change. As you waken your worthiness, you have the opportunity to reframe the way you view change. You were inherently born with the highest expression of life's joys inside you. What if embracing change as a positive could improve the quality of your life?

Change is coming one way or another. Embrace the uncomfortable with curiosity and a sense of wonder and choose to change. Choose to pursue your inner callings. Point your choices in the direction of your deepest desires and watch as life unfolds in the most beautiful and supportive ways.

Embracing Change as a Positive

What does it mean to bear-hug what's uncomfortable? It means fully embracing and accepting the challenges, uncertainties, and discomforts that come with personal growth and development. It involves recognizing that stepping out of your comfort zone is essential for unlocking your true potential and living a life that truly reflects your values and capabilities.

It is essential to understand that discomfort is often a sign of growth. It's the body's and mind's initial reaction to new situations, challenges, and opportunities that push us beyond our usual boundaries. Yet we can choose to actively seek out and engage in situations that challenge us, rather than avoiding them. This could mean taking on new responsibilities, trying new things, or even changing behaviors and habits that no longer serve our best interests.

Bear-hugging uncomfortable experiences leverages them as learning opportunities. It means reflecting on what these situations teach about yourself, your values, and your needs, and how you can use this knowledge to further align your life with your inherent worth. Living authentically often requires facing societal pressures or expectations. These may be uncomfortable to break away from, but doing so allows you to express your true self, which is part of your return to radiance.

For example, Cassie, the mother of three kids, was the primary breadwinner in her family. Her husband was supportive, but his career was not as lucrative as Cassie's. Cassie felt frustrated in her sales role because she was just clearing six figures, but she knew she was worth more and she wasn't using her strengths to her full ability. The thought of changing jobs felt scary to both Cassie and her husband, so she stayed and tolerated the job despite her inner calling to align her work with her worth and talent.

Then one day Cassie had the courage to mention her situation to a friend in the same industry. Cassie feared that saying she was underpaid and underutilized in her current role would come across as arrogant. However, the opposite happened. Her friend also recognized the value of her contributions and agreed with her. Cassie's friend also mentioned that the sparkle in Cassie's eyes had been missing and it might be time to start looking.

This conversation empowered Cassie to approach change differently. She saw change as a positive and necessary thing to become aligned with her worthiness and her values. Her husband agreed, and Cassie took the next steps to look for a new role. One positive action stacked on top of another, one step at a time, and within two months, Cassie found a new role that doubled her income and aligned with her strengths and talents. As a result, her relationships, health, and happiness improved, too.

Cassie took intentional steps to bear-hug uncomfortable and to embrace change with curiosity and a sense of wonder. Cassie's story serves as an invitation to create change in a way that is less scary and more exciting.

Here are some steps you can take to bear-hug what's uncomfortable with less stress and more optimism:

- Define what matters: Having a clear understanding of your objectives can motivate you to push through discomfort. What matters to you most and why is it important to you?

- Set micro goals: Focus on completing one step at a time, rather than overwhelming yourself with the entire process. How can you break the task or goal into smaller, more manageable steps?
- Focus on benefits: Whether it's personal growth, improved relationships, or career advancement, keeping the long-term benefits in mind can help you stay motivated. What benefits will you receive by taking action even if it's uncomfortable?
- Practice self-compassion: Instead of berating yourself for feeling uncomfortable, practice self-compassion and remind yourself that it's OK to feel this way. How can you be kind to yourself? What can you acknowledge about yourself for trying despite the discomfort?
- Use positive affirmations: Repeat phrases like "I am capable," "I am resilient," and "I can do hard things." These help bolster self-belief. What other positive affirmations could you use to shift your mindset and boost your confidence?
- Seek positive support: Having someone to encourage and cheer you on can make facing discomfort feel less daunting. Who do you know in your circle of friends, family, and colleagues who could help mentor you through uncomfortable yet positive changes?

Inherently Worthy

Imagine yourself as a multimillionaire. Imagine you have everything you ever wanted. You are living the glamorous life, and you get to experience all the luxuries life has to offer. Where are you and what are you doing? Are you on a yacht, in a mansion on the beach, or traveling in a private jet? How are you harnessing your uniqueness and making a massive impact in the world? What does it look like and how does it feel?

The good news is this reality is possible for you! Maybe your dream isn't to be a multimillionaire. Success shouldn't be defined by what we have but rather by how we feel. The point is you are worthy of a beautiful life just because you exist.

When you embrace the idea that optimized health, wealth, happiness, and fulfillment are your inherent rights, defining what this optimized vision of your worth looks like becomes a deeply personal exploration. Once identified, this can empower you to bear-hug uncomfortable in your spiritual growth.

Here are ten questions to help you explore and define what new levels of worthiness look like for you:

1. What does a fulfilling day look like to you? Reflect on the activities, interactions, and accomplishments that leave you feeling satisfied and fulfilled. This can help you understand what elements are essential for your daily success.

2. How do you want to feel most of the time? Identify the emotions you want to experience regularly — such as joy, peace, empowerment, and connectedness — which can guide your decisions and help you prioritize what truly matters.

3. What are your core values, and how can your actions align more closely with these values? Knowing your core values allows you to live authentically and make choices that bring you closer to your vision of success. What values did you name in POWER Up Your Practice 7: Your Top Values (page 72)?

4. What does health mean to you, and what habits support your optimal health? Define what good health looks like for you, considering physical, mental, and emotional aspects, and identify the practices that support this state.

5. What kind of wealth do you want to accumulate, and

why? Consider what wealth means to you beyond financial abundance. It might include relationships, experiences, knowledge, or spiritual richness.

6. What achievements would make you proud, and why are these achievements important? Think about what accomplishments would genuinely make you feel successful and understand why they hold significance in your life.

7. How do you want to impact your community and the world, and what steps can you take to make this impact? Reflect on your desired legacy and the mark you wish to leave on the world, which can define your path to success.

8. Who do you admire for their success, and what qualities do they have that you can emulate? Identifying role models and the traits they possess can provide a road map for personal and professional development.

9. How can you balance ambition with contentment? Explore ways to pursue your goals vigorously while also appreciating your current achievements and circumstances.

10. What barriers do you face when it comes to acknowledging your worthiness, and how can you overcome them? Recognize any self-limiting beliefs or external challenges that hinder your acceptance of your inherent worth and strategize ways to address these barriers.

These questions encourage deep reflection and are designed to help you define your worthiness in a way that is aligned with your highest self. By considering these aspects, you can create a personalized and holistic vision of success that enriches your life and aligns with your belief in your inherent worthiness. This empowers you to embrace change with a sense of positive curiosity and a willingness to take action.

Grab Your Gemstone: Every step you take to embrace change with a bear hug of excitement and wonder helps you recognize your inherent worth and adds richness and depth to your life. It connects you to your radiance and gives you a sense of agency over your choices. Bear-hug uncomfortable with courage, and let your inherent worth shine brightly as you spread your wings and soar.

POWER Thought: I AM WORTHY!

POWER Up Your Practice 13: "I Am Worthy of Change" Commitment Statement

Use this exercise to help give you a boost of commitment and courage to embrace change as a positive — knowing that it will lead to empowering and beautiful outcomes when done with intention. Either say this out loud to yourself, or retype it, or copy it, sign it, and post it where you can see it.

I, _____, commit to embracing the winds of change with a heart full of wonder and a spirit ignited by excitement. I recognize that each change, whether big or small, is a stepping stone toward the full realization of my true potential and inherent worth. I pledge to view each shift in my life as an opportunity to grow, learn, and expand my horizons.

I vow to nurture my health, enrich my experiences, and expand my understanding, knowing that these are the foundations of the wealth and happiness I seek. With each day, I will take actions that align with my deepest values, fostering fulfillment and joy in my journey.

I am open to the possibilities that change brings and am ready to adapt with enthusiasm and confidence. I will celebrate each moment of success and learn from every challenge, using them as fuel to propel me toward my goals.

Through this commitment, I am declaring that I am worthy of a life filled with love, success, and satisfaction. I embrace the beautiful unfolding of my destiny, ready to shine in my full radiance and to influence the world positively.

This is my vow to myself, made with clarity and purpose, to live every day as a testament to my inherent worthiness.

Signature:
Date:

CHAPTER FOURTEEN

Unlock Abundance

*D*o you ever wonder why some people seem to have more abundance than others? Is it luck, charm, hard work, birth status? From a material-wealth perspective, it could be one of these or a combination. From the perspective of personal radiance, I am talking about abundance on a soul level. This can manifest in a variety of ways, such as wealth, health, relationships, opportunities, love, energy, and an overall feeling that life is working for us rather than against us.

What does abundance mean to you? Just like being born makes us inherently worthy of everything we have ever dreamed or desired, we are inherently abundant regardless of our current status. The goal of this chapter is to help you unlock abundance and align your worthiness with the truth that all is already yours. Once you define what abundance means to you, then you signal to the Universe that this is what you are trying to create. Infinite Intelligence gets excited because it gets to deliver what is already meant to be yours. It just needs direction and permission to move into action.

Worth and wealth have a direct correlation. Your wealth and abundance will mirror your internal levels of self-worth. This is why wakening your worthiness is such an important part of returning to your radiance because deep down your self-worth needs to be high for you to receive all the blessings and bliss that life has to offer.

What Do You Wish For?

Pretend you were Aladdin with the magic lamp in your hands. You rub this magic lamp and poof! Out comes a genie to grant you three wishes. As in the story, asking for more wishes isn't an option, and in this case, the wishes have to be for yourself. What do you wish for? A million dollars, to meet the love of your life, a mansion on the beach, perfect health, record-breaking success in business? I encourage you to pause now and consider what three things you would wish for.

According to MakeWish.org, here are the top wishes people make: health and longevity, love and companionship, and success and financial stability. Do any of your wishes fall into these categories? For these wishes to come true, you need to feel that you are worthy of receiving them. What prevents wishes for abundance from coming true is our inability to feel like we deserve them.

Feeling like we deserve abundance is crucial for receiving it because of the psychological and energetic implications that shape how we interact with the world. Here are several reasons why this mindset is important:

- Self-worth and receptivity: Believing that we deserve abundance is inherently tied to self-worth. When we feel worthy, we are more open to receiving good things, whether that's opportunities, relationships, wealth, or other forms of success. If we don't believe we deserve these things, we might unconsciously reject them or sabotage our own efforts.
- Positive expectations: Expecting positive outcomes can influence what happens in our lives, a principle often discussed in the law of attraction. Feeling deserving of abundance encourages a positive outlook, which can attract positive circumstances and people.
- Motivation and action: Believing we deserve abundance

can motivate us to take the actions necessary to achieve it. It drives the pursuit of goals with confidence and persistence, rather than hesitation and doubt.

- Overcoming limiting beliefs: Many people have deep-seated limiting beliefs about their worthiness that can block abundance. Recognizing and feeling that we deserve abundance is a vital step in overcoming these beliefs and allowing ourselves to pursue and accept prosperity.
- Enhanced decision-making: When we feel deserving of abundance, we are more likely to make choices that align with this belief. This might include pursuing higher-paying job opportunities, investing in personal development, or establishing boundaries that protect our time and energy.
- Relationship dynamics: Feeling deserving of abundance also affects how we interact in relationships. It enables us to seek out and nurture relationships that are reciprocal and enriching, rather than those that may be draining or unfulfilling.
- Quality of life: Ultimately, feeling deserving of abundance isn't just about material wealth or external success; it's about allowing ourselves to live a fulfilling life. This perspective opens us up to experiences and joys that enrich our lives and foster a sense of completeness.

Feeling that we deserve abundance is essential for our wishes to come true because it influences our psychological state, behaviors, and the way we interact with the Universe. It's a foundational belief that supports living a fuller, more-satisfying life.

The Power of Gratitude

This book describes many techniques to improve your sense of self-worth, such as positive affirmations and mantras, visualizations, journaling, mindfulness, and so on. However, practicing gratitude is a surefire way to elevate your emotions and frequency and to align with abundance. In other words, if you want your wishes to come true, it helps to focus on the wishes that have already been granted.

Gratitude journaling is a powerful tool for enhancing the belief that you deserve abundance, bliss, and blessings. In a journal, use these questions and prompts to guide you to reflect on your worthiness and to reinforce a positive mindset. While you can focus on the past, focus in particular on today:

- The abundance all around: What abundance did you notice in your life today? This could be material, emotional, spiritual, or relational.
- Gifts of the day: What unexpected blessings or gifts did you receive today? How do you feel about receiving these?
- Joyful moments: What moments of joy did you experience today? What made these moments special?
- Self-compliments: What are three things you love about yourself? How do these qualities contribute to your life and to others?
- Daily generosity: In what ways were you generous today? How does giving make you feel about your own abundance?
- Manifestations coming to life: What are some desires or goals that are beginning to manifest in your life? How do these manifestations make you feel about your future?
- Reflections on the past: When have you felt most abundant in your life? Describe what inspired those feelings and how you can invite more of that into your current life.
- People who lift you up: Who makes you feel loved and valued? How do their actions reinforce your belief in your worthiness?
- Affirmations of worth: Write down three affirmations that

reinforce your worthiness of bliss, abundance, and blessings. Why do you believe these affirmations are true?

- Dreams for the future: What are your dreams for the future? Why are you worthy of these dreams becoming reality?

Aligned Action vs. Proving It to Earn It

Heidi was in her first corporate leadership position and newly married. Heidi was smart and hardworking. She grew up playing sports and loved to prove people wrong, especially if they thought she couldn't do something. This was a strength of Heidi's when it came to winning because she dug deep down into her character and tapped into her resilience, determination, and perseverance. When she proved she could do something, it made the satisfaction of earning whatever it was ten times greater.

When it came to the game of life, however, Heidi's prove-it-to-earn-it formula didn't seem to work as well. Heidi wanted to be a loving wife, and to prove that she loved her husband and thought about him often, she would shower him with both small and lavish gifts. Her husband, on the other hand, although he appreciated the gifts, wanted her time and presence — not presents.

As a sales leader, Heidi knew that the more sales she and her team generated, the more money she would make. She also wanted to prove to her leadership team that they had made the right decision in promoting her. Heidi took it upon herself to come in early and work late to satisfy her desires for a loving marriage, to earn more money, and to have a validating career.

To Heidi's dismay, her plan backfired. Her husband became more distant rather than closer, since he felt that she prioritized work over him. This felt confusing to Heidi. In essence, the reason she worked so much was for him. Work also wasn't going the way she expected. Working long days left her in a state of fatigue that impacted her results. Despite her committed schedule of extra hours, her team was not one of the top-producing teams. This forced Heidi to define her wishes and ask herself if her actions aligned with the abundant outcomes she desired. When she did this, she realized they did not.

Where do you think Heidi went wrong? Like many of us, Heidi was trying to prove her worth and value. Her plan failed because, in the eyes of the Universe, Heidi was already a loving wife and career badass — she did not need to prove it. The act of proving it to earn it told the Universe that Heidi did not believe she was these things, and until she believed, Infinite Intelligence could not deliver the outcome she wanted.

As you waken your worthiness and unlock abundance for yourself, it's important to take aligned action rather than trying to prove it to earn it. The moment you believe you have to prove that you are worthy of, or have to earn, something before you can receive it, you are out of alignment with the Universe's abundance frequency. Proving is a human and earthly concept that has value only in the right setting. Proving is not a cosmic or Universe-based concept because it indicates that you are not yet the thing that the Universe knows you to be. Infinite Intelligence responds to aligned action, which means your actions are aligned with the truth from the Universe's perspective that you already are worthy and abundant.

The goal is to align our actions to mirror someone who is already in receipt of the thing that they wish or desire to the best of their ability. We are souls in a human body, and we are also human beings housing a soul within. I say this because our human condition can prevent us from acting as if. If that feels like the case for you, visualize or do what you can to act as if. The cool part about working with the Universe is that it is boundless, so it responds to your energy and not your physical abilities — much can be generated by simply embodying and visualizing your desired abundance as received.

To help you align your actions, a fun game you can play is what I call "If I Already." This has helped many of my clients and students unlock abundance.

The game goes like this:

- Name one of your wishes. For example: I wish I had a million dollars.
- Next, imagine the wish was granted and ask: If I already was a millionaire, how would my actions look different?
- List the actions you would take. In this example, that might be to flip properties, invest in hedge funds and the stock market, hire professionals to maximize your money, start your own business, and so on.
- Next, list the actions you can take — including embodying the feeling of your wish being fulfilled — to align with the outcomes you seek.
- Finally, start taking inspired action as if this desire is already yours. Why? Because in the eyes of the Universe, you were born worthy, deserving, and abundant.

Grab Your Gemstone: Your sense of worth and the belief you deserve abundance are deeply interconnected. Material wealth and external success are just one aspect of abundance, which at its core is about a soul-level experience of wealth that manifests as health, relationships, opportunities, love, and energy. Recognizing that you are inherently worthy and abundant, regardless of current circumstances, is crucial for unlocking the Universe's riches.

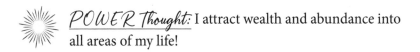

POWER Thought: I attract wealth and abundance into all areas of my life!

POWER Up Your Practice 14: The Har Haray Haree Wahe Guru Mantra

A powerful Kundalini yoga mantra for unlocking abundance and attracting bliss is the Har Haray Haree Wahe Guru mantra. This mantra is often used to manifest prosperity and creative energy in one's life. It's considered very effective in wakening your worthiness to receive abundance and experience the joy of the Universe's infinite blessings.

Here's the meaning of the mantra:

- Har: This word is often associated with the creative aspect of the Universe. It is meant to burn away ego and the negativity that blocks us from our divine nature.
- Haray: Another form of Har, this represents the flow or manifestation of the divine in the physical world.
- Haree: A celebration or sealing of the divine manifestation; it finalizes the process, ensuring that the creative energy is delivered.
- Wahe Guru: This statement of awe and ecstasy translates to "wonderful Teacher." It celebrates the divine wisdom and enlightenment bestowed by the Universe.

For maximum results, I recommend incorporating this mantra into your daily meditation practice. This can help you feel more connected to the flow of abundance and bliss. When you are ready to chant, take a seated position with your spine straight, eyes closed, and hands in Gyan Mudra (index finger and thumb touching). Ideally, chant this mantra 108 times, which is equivalent to completing a full round of a mala bead necklace. Using a mala helps focus the mind and intensify the meditation experience. If you don't have a mala, just chant the mantra for a set amount of time, but at least for eleven counts.

If you chant the mantra slowly and meditatively, this helps calm the mind, while chanting more quickly energizes the spirit and body.

By regularly chanting this mantra, you affirm your openness to receive abundance and express bliss, aligning your energy with the Universe's inherent gifts for you. The vibrations from chanting clear blockages in the energy pathways, allowing prosperity and happiness to flow freely into your life.

CHAPTER FIFTEEN

Believe It to See It

We have the incredible gift of visualizing the experiences and outcomes that we desire and bringing them into existence. How cool is that? When we embody those visualizations and activate all five of our senses, we waken our worthiness and attract that which we desire. The limitless part of us begins interacting with Infinite Intelligence. This brings into manifestation the very thing that we have been dreaming about.

Professional athletes embrace this ability to reach superhuman results all the time, and you can, too. How different could your life be if you embraced full sensory visualization until you embodied it as your truth? By taking the time to envision your desires until you feel them as truth, you tell your subconscious mind that what you want is not only possible but also something you are truly capable of achieving. You train your mind to focus on the positive outcomes you want and to let go of any negative self-talk or doubt that might hold you back.

Believe It to See It

Muhammad Ali once said, "If my mind can conceive it, and my heart can believe it — then I can achieve it." This quote really captures the truth that if we get out of a limited mindset, anything is possible.

Your soul already knows you are the very thing you wish to be and that you are capable of achieving anything you truly desire. It doesn't need to believe it — it needs you to believe it. Your radiance already contains all your gifts, talents, strengths, and everything you will ever need to rise to the fullness of your potential. When you believe it, your soul and your radiance will light up that cosmic connection between you and Infinite Intelligence to bring into reality the thing you have been visualizing.

When you visualize it, you will believe it. When you believe it, you will see it. Some of our most celebrated athletes, movie stars, and pop icons have practiced the art of visualizing their outcomes, feeling and embodying the goal as already accomplished. When they visualize or imagine a successful completion of their desire with full sensory embodiment, many claim to have seen their stardom unfold before their very eyes. Famous actor Jim Carrey tells the story of how, early in his career, he wrote himself a check for ten million dollars and kept it in his wallet. A couple years later, he received that exact amount when he signed the contract for the movie *The Mask*.

There are tons of famous examples of this. At one point, average ordinary people became extraordinary in their craft because they committed to the practice of visualizing until they believed it. If you committed to this practice, what could your health look like? Your wealth? Your relationships? How could this practice unlock new opportunities for you?

Envision Victory

As a teenager, I played competitive soccer, and I remember once getting ready to play in the state championships. I used a five-sensory visualization to prepare for the game before I even knew it was a technique. This was something I did regularly as a soccer player.

Before practice or a game, I arrived early, especially if it was a morning game. The smell of the grass and the quietness of the field set the scene and helped me to go within. I stepped onto the field, facing the goal box, in the spot where I would practice goal-scoring kicks. Then I closed my eyes and felt the wind on my face. It felt as if the wind were supporting me in my efforts to be my best. With my eyes closed, I envisioned the intensity of needing to score the winning point. I imagined the goalie doing everything in their power to deflect my shot. I felt the pressure from my coach and my teammates knowing that the responsibility to win was on me.

I pretended to hear the crowd cheering me on and other fans shouting for the opposing team to block me. I engaged my sense of taste as I imagined the sweat dripping down my face and its salty essence touching my lips. Smelling the grass of the soccer field was always comforting to me, since I knew I was exactly where I was supposed to be.

Before the state championship, I envisioned the moment in my mind. I visualized my final face-off with the goalie, my fake-out maneuver, stepping back, and making the kick. GOOOOAAAAL! Victory pulsed through my entire being as the sounds of family and friends celebrating from the bleachers filled my ears. I imagined my coaches approaching with pride and the team leaping into a tearful embrace of joy and relief. We did it, we won the championship!

When I opened my eyes, I fully embraced the energy and the experience. I knew in my bones that if I were responsible for scoring that winning goal, I could lead the team to victory. During the championship, this envisioning proved to be beneficial: I successfully scored two goals that helped the team to victory, as we won the game by a score of four to three.

You can be victorious, too. Whether you want to master a sport, improve your health, bring a dream into reality, build your business, or find the perfect partner, the possibilities to apply five-sensory visualization are endless.

Making It Real

Five-sensory visualization activates neurons in the body by engaging multiple neural networks, evoking emotions, creating new neural pathways, influencing the subconscious mind, and impacting the endocrine system, which regulates hormones. Through consistent practice and belief in the power of visualization, you can harness this ability to manifest your goals and improve your overall well-being.

Incorporate all five senses into any visualization meditation (like the one in this chapter), as this can truly elevate your practice and help you own your outcomes and your opportunities. Here's a guide to help you engage each sense so you can maximize your experience:

SIGHT

- Imagine yourself in a specific place or scenario aligned with your visualization goal, allowing vivid details to unfold.
- Envision the colors, shapes, textures, and movements around you with remarkable clarity.
- Picture specific objects, individuals, or scenes symbolizing the achievement of your desired outcome.
- Visualize yourself attaining your goal, capturing the expressions, gestures, and actions associated with success.

SOUND

- Listen intently to the sounds resonating with your visualization, whether it's the melodies of nature, soothing music, or empowering affirmations.
- Create an auditory landscape reflecting your desired scenario, including background noises, conversations, or supportive statements tailored to your goal.

- Infuse your visualization with positive affirmations or uplifting messages that deeply resonate with you.

TOUCH

- Immerse yourself in the tactile sensations linked to your visualization, embracing the textures of objects, surfaces, or materials.
- Feel the warmth of the sun caressing your skin, the softness of fabric against your fingertips, or the sensation of gentle movement.
- Envision physical interactions, such as handshakes, embraces, or gestures of encouragement, igniting a profound sense of connection and support.

TASTE

- Envision the flavors associated with your visualization, indulging in the tastes of delightful foods, beverages, or other elements that bring you joy and satisfaction.
- Integrate the sensation of taste into your visualization, relishing in the exquisite pleasure it brings to your imagined scenario and allowing taste to enhance your mental experience.

SMELL

- Recall familiar scents and aromas relevant to your visualization, whether it's the fragrance of nature, blossoming flowers, or beloved culinary delights.
- Imagine the aromatic essence that permeates your surroundings, from the crisp freshness of the air to a subtle perfume lingering in the breeze.
- Engage your sense of smell by visualizing specific scents that evoke feelings of happiness, tranquility, or inspiration, enhancing the depth of your meditation.

By embracing these sensory elements in your visualization practice, you can create a profoundly connected experience that activates numerous neural and cosmic pathways. This amplifies the impact of your meditation and further wakens your worthiness to align your outcomes to your desires. Explore different combinations to discover what resonates most deeply with you and empowers you to manifest your desires into reality. This process connects you to your radiance and the infinite possibilities that await you.

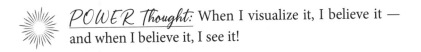 *Grab Your Gemstone:* The ability to visualize and manifest your desires to align with your inherent worth is within you. This practice of visualizing symbolizes something profound — the infinite potential you hold to create your own reality and bring your dreams to fruition. Through the power of visualization, you tap into your cosmic connections and unlock the beautiful outcomes of Infinite Intelligence, shaping your destiny with unwavering belief and the intention that you deserve and are worthy of a wonderful life.

POWER Thought: When I visualize it, I believe it — and when I believe it, I see it!

POWER Up Your Practice 15: Five-Sensory Visualization Meditation

Your soul is waiting for you to connect with it in such a way that it awakens all that you were born to be. This five-sensory visualization meditation is the cosmic bridge between where you are and where you dream to be.

Before you begin, prepare for this experience. Name the outcome you are visualizing along with how that will be experienced by your five senses:

1. What are you visualizing and what positive outcome does it embody?
2. What do you see when you do this?
3. What do you hear?
4. What do you taste?
5. What do you feel?
6. What do you smell?

Once you know what you intend to visualize, sit or lie down in a comfortable position where you won't be interrupted, then begin:

*   Close your eyes and take a few deep breaths. On the exhale, mentally say to yourself, *Clear, clear, clear.* This assists in clearing the mind and reaching a relaxed state.
*   Start to visualize the activity or achieving the desired outcome. Keep your eyes closed and breathe deeply throughout as you envision all the details.
*   First, what do you see? What colors, shapes, and textures are around you? What does the scene look like? Who is with you? Take it all in.
*   Next, focus on the sounds. What do you hear? Is it the sounds of nature? Applause? The voice of loved ones? Focus on environmental noises. Allow yourself to hear everything loudly.
*   Next, engage your sense of touch. Are you holding anything? Are you touching something or someone? Do you feel wind or sunshine on your face? Are there handshakes, warm embraces, or physical activity? As you deepen into your experience, really feel everything that happens.
*   Remember to keep breathing deeply as you enter the world of taste. Are foods and drinks part of this experience? Can you "taste" your victory? Can you taste the air?
*   Next, focus on the sense of smell. Invite the aromas and the fragrances around you. Are there pleasant smells of incense, oils, or perfumes? Do you smell food? Do you smell

the forest, the ocean, or other aspects of nature? Do you smell the familiar scent of a loved one? Visualize all the smells that might exist.

- Finally, bring together all the senses for a full embodiment of the experience. Allow yourself to feel the electrifying and satisfying emotions of reaching this goal, accomplishment, or desire. Savor the moment and take it all in. Breathe deeply and with pride, knowing that you are capable of this.
- When you feel ready, gently bring your focus back to the present. Take another deep breath and release the visualization. Express gratitude for this incredible opportunity to engage in this mental and spiritual rehearsal, since the potential it unlocks is infinite. Know that you are equipped with both the mental and physical prowess to succeed.

And when those eyes of yours flutter open, carry that positive energy, that unwavering confidence, into every moment of your day. Trust in your abilities, for you have prepared yourself inside and out for the success that awaits.

Adapt this visualization to fit your needs. Embrace what resonates with you, and create a vivid experience that ignites your passion, focus, and unwavering belief in yourself — because once you visualize it, you believe it, and then get ready because soon you'll see it.

PART FOUR

ELEVATE YOUR
Energy

The higher your energy level, the more efficient
your body. The more efficient your body, the better
you feel and the more you will use your talent
to produce outstanding results.

— TONY ROBBINS

CHAPTER SIXTEEN

The Yoga of Self-Awareness

According to a 2024 Pew Research Center study, 64 percent of US adults said they spend time each month looking inward or centering themselves. Most of them — 44 percent — say they do this primarily to feel connected with their true self, with something bigger than themselves, and with other people. This means that almost two-thirds of the US population is seeking to return to their radiance.

Part 4 of the POWER Method focuses on elevating your energy using teachings from the transformative practice of Kundalini yoga. I've mentioned Kundalini a few times already, but now we'll take a deeper dive. Kundalini techniques can be practiced independently or combined in whatever way works best for you.

This chapter focuses on the overall science of Kundalini yoga, its framework, and how we can leverage it in our everyday lives to help return to our radiance and stay in it. We do this by accessing the transformational power of energy centers, breathwork, mantras, and meditation.

Awakening Kundalini Energy

Kundalini yoga is the yoga of self-awareness due to its profound focus on awakening and harnessing kundalini energy — a dormant energy at the base of the spine that is believed to be the source of spiritual enlightenment. I refer to this energy as our inner and personal power.

Kundalini yoga uses a combination of physical postures, energy centers, breathing techniques, meditation, and the chanting of mantras to cultivate and elevate this energy, fostering a deep connection between the physical and cosmic realms. This powerful technology's blended, purposeful, systematic approach is based on the laws of science, psychology, and metaphysics, and it awakens our true potential and is a gateway to higher consciousness.

Here's why Kundalini yoga is seen as a significant technological system in the realm of spiritual practices and how it works when you incorporate it into your life:

- Holistic activation: Kundalini yoga engages on multiple levels — physical, mental, emotional, and spiritual. This holistic approach helps us become more aware of our inner states and how these states influence our overall well-being.

- Energy centers: This practice places significant emphasis on the chakras, or energy centers, which are thought to be vital for our life force. By focusing on activating and balancing these chakras, practitioners gain a deeper understanding of their energetic body, leading to greater self-awareness and spiritual growth.

- Transformational potential: Kundalini yoga is known for its potential to bring about rapid personal transformation. As the kundalini energy — our personal power — gets activated and rises from the base of the spine through the crown, it is said to illuminate the true nature of the practitioner, revealing inherent strengths and areas for growth and returning them to their radiance.

- Intensive meditation and mantras: The use of dynamic meditations and specific mantras in Kundalini yoga helps to quiet the mind and sharpen focus. Deep meditation leads to heightened self-awareness and an enhanced ability to observe our thoughts and emotions objectively. Mantras help activate what we want to bring into our world and distance us from what does not serve us.

- Emphasis on experience: This practice encourages an experiential understanding of our sense of self and the Universe. Through regular practice, we learn to experience and integrate the teachings personally, rather than through intellectual study alone. We learn to trust the messages our intuition and our body are telling us, leading us to a more aligned and harmonic life.

- Physical and psychic development: The practice includes kriyas — specific sequences of poses and breathing exercises designed to build physical vitality and increase awareness. As health and awareness improve, a deeper understanding of the self emerges that allows us to embrace more of who we are, including our gifts, talents, and strengths.

- Release of blockages: Kundalini yoga helps identify and release blockages in both our physical and radiant bodies. This release is often accompanied by significant emotional processing, which fosters a greater understanding of our personal emotional landscapes and their impact on our lives.

By consistently practicing Kundalini yoga and its various aspects, you can cultivate a deep sense of self-awareness that guides you toward spiritual awakening, fulfillment, happiness, and optimized health. Ultimately, this unleashes your true potential.

The Ten Bodies: The Foundational Framework

The ten bodies is the fundamental framework of Kundalini yoga that explains the multidimensional aspects of human existence and how tapping into them can positively impact our lives. The ten bodies includes the physical body, three mental bodies, and six energy bodies. This comprehensive framework allows us to work on multiple levels of our being, addressing our physical, mental, and spiritual aspects simultaneously.

By understanding the ten bodies, Kundalini yoga offers deeper insight into various aspects of our radiance. If you have tried traditional therapies and remedies to solve discomfort and disconnection and you still feel off, consider using this model to reconnect to your true self. Each body has its specific functions and characteristics, and their harmonious integration enhances our overall well-being and spiritual growth. Imbalances in any of these bodies can lead to physical, emotional, or spiritual issues, which is why this framework is so extraordinary, since each body can help heal and restore.

Another important aspect of the ten bodies is that everything in Kundalini yoga — from the exercises to the meditations and everything in between — is designed to activate and balance these bodies, promoting maximized health and vitality. Kundalini techniques optimize the ten bodies and help us gain insight into our behaviors, patterns, and the deeper layers of our psyche. This awareness is crucial for personal transformation and the ability to manifest into reality the fullness of our potential.

Here are the ten bodies:

1. Soul Body: This connects us to our eternal identity beyond physical existence and fosters a strong desire to follow our dreams and bliss.

2. Negative Mind: The second body provides protection and caution, helping to assess risks. Its goal is to overcome the negative to build meaningful relationships and to merge with community.

3. Positive Mind: This represents our expansive nature, which sees the positive aspects of situations. Its

motivation is to restore hope and faith in others and to see the world through optimistic eyes.

4. Neutral Mind: The fourth body allows for balanced and wise decision-making, integrating the inputs from the Positive Mind and the Negative Mind. Its goal is to seek calmness and clarity in our inner and outer worlds.

5. Physical Body: The fifth body deals with physical health and the ability to enjoy physical existence. It inspires a deep drive to share our gifts and talents to uplift others.

6. Arcline: This is the home of our intuition and willpower. Its strong desire is to create our own reality by our own design.

7. Aura: The seventh body is the electromagnetic field that provides protection and projection. We feel drawn to uplift and nurture ourselves and others.

8. Pranic Body: This governs the breath and life-force energy. It creates a strong desire to be connected to the infinite and limitless source of energy and possibilities.

9. Subtle Body: The ninth body allows for the subtle and nuanced understanding of deeper spiritual truths. It motivates us to understand the seen and unseen, to see the big picture, and clearly communicate all we know.

10. Radiant Body: The tenth body relates to royalty, radiance, and the courage to live out our truth and potential. We feel the extreme desire to express our potential with excellence and inspire others to do the same.

Practicing the Kundalini techniques in part 4 will help you understand and harmonize these ten bodies, and this will bring about a profound transformation that aligns your physical life with your potential, your purpose, and your capabilities to elevate your energy and help you live life fully.

Tap into the Ten Bodies

Imagine a life that is full of energy and vitality. Where your strengths, gifts, and talents shine brightly for the world to see. From this state, you elevate your impact and make a positive difference in the world by just being you. That's what's available by developing a deeper understanding of the ten bodies.

Below, I provide a more detailed description of the ten bodies. For each, I outline their purpose, the qualities that indicate when we are in alignment with that body and when we are out of alignment, a pose to practice that relates to that body, and a motto to use as an affirmation. In this chapter's POWER Up Your Practice, I give instructions for each of the ten poses. Tapping into the ten bodies will help you return to radiance with more velocity and vitality.

Body 1: Soul Body

The Soul Body, often referred to as the Soul, embodies the essence of who we truly are beyond the physical and mental realms. It serves as our unwavering compass, guiding us through life's complexities with clarity and purpose. Connecting with our Soul allows us to align with our deepest truths and divine potential, leading to a harmonious existence in alignment with our higher calling.

SOUL BODY AT A GLANCE

- Purpose: Your Soul is on it and is taking lead. Connect with it, and suddenly, life isn't this confusing maze anymore. You've got a GPS straight to your calling.
- In alignment: Intellect and emotion are balanced; you relate to inner self and radiate vitality, compassion, and steadiness.
- Out of alignment: You are overintellectual, sympathetic versus compassionate, deny feeling, have a lack of self-love, and are inconsistent.

- Pose to practice: Lotus pose
- Motto: I follow my bliss!

Body 2: Negative Mind

The Negative Mind diligently safeguards our well-being. As a vital component of our mental architecture alongside the Positive Mind and the Neutral Mind, it forms a crucial trio in orchestrating our inner harmony. Far from merely dwelling on pessimism, the Negative Mind serves as our astute guardian, evaluating risks, anticipating challenges, and prioritizing our safety. When faced with critical choices, it offers invaluable discernment, guiding us toward informed decisions.

NEGATIVE MIND AT A GLANCE

- Purpose: It helps you stay Sherlock-sharp, objectively examining situations, people, and events to fully grasp their implications.
- In alignment: You possess situational awareness, practical decision-making, strong community, the ability to take calculated risks, and the ability to set healthy boundaries.
- Out of alignment: You feel a longing to belong, leading to self-abandonment, overprotectiveness, insecurity, indecisiveness, and having a hard time seeing positive outcomes.
- Pose to practice: Bear grip
- Motto: My discernment helps me reach my full potential.

Body 3: Positive Mind

The Positive Mind is an integral member of the mental trio devoted to nurturing optimism and fortitude. Beyond mere optimism, it stands for hope and resilience, guiding us through life's trials with unwavering faith in brighter horizons. However, it's essential to blend positivity with discernment, steering clear of potential pitfalls. Our Positive Mind serves as a wise navigator, leading us toward purpose, contentment, and assurance amid life's complexities.

Positive Mind at a Glance

- Purpose: This keeps your hopes and dreams alive and nurtures the unwavering belief that when all seems lost, your spirit, resilience, and determination can still light the path forward.
- In alignment: You project light and hope to others, have a good sense of humor and boundless determination, and are uplifting, optimistic, and action-oriented.
- Out of alignment: You display unrealistic expectations, people-pleasing behavior, ignorance toward danger, and hopelessness and self-destructiveness.
- Pose to practice: Stretch pose
- Motto: Life says yes to me and I say yes to life!

Body 4: Neutral Mind

The Neutral Mind offers profound insights, steadfast calm, and wise choices. When cultivated, our Neutral Mind illuminates our path in clarity. Yet when we're not tuned in to it we can have roadblocks and rigidity. The Neutral Mind provides intuitive revelations, enlightening revelations, and even extraordinary occurrences.

Neutral Mind at a Glance

- Purpose: Think of it as the Zen master of your mental crew, keeping you levelheaded during the ups and downs of life.
- In alignment: You feel steadiness, calm under pressure,

invisible to outside influence, intuitive, and clearheaded; are a great listener; and experience spiritual growth.
- Out of alignment: You experience stubbornness, arrogance, radical thoughts and concepts, and limited personal growth, and you feel stuck.
- Pose to practice: Easy pose with Gyan Mudra and Sodarshan Chakra Kriya
- Motto: When I meditate, I elevate!

Body 5: Physical Body

Our Physical Body is more than just a body; it's a vessel in which we express ourselves to the world, earning it the nickname "the Teacher." Beyond its outward appearance and health, it embodies our personal power and resilience. When in harmony, it can propel us into careers that capitalize on our physical capabilities. Yet when disruptions occur, they may trigger bouts of self-doubt and fluctuations in energy. Our body's innate ability to impart wisdom and lead others comes from this body. Embrace its strength, vitality, and endurance.

PHYSICAL BODY AT A GLANCE

- Purpose: To be your earthly chariot, your vessel for exploring this wild, wonderful world in self-expression, strength, and service to others.
- In alignment: You own your strengths and talents, have high self-regard, are in tune with the body and its messages, are a great teacher or instructor, and have strong vitality and boundless energy.
- Out of alignment: You go to extremes, either showing obsessive care or low regard for the body. You may be self-critical, lack personal agency, dismiss your strengths, and become hyperfocused on flaws.

- Pose to practice: Frog pose
- Motto: I love my body!

Body 6: Arcline

The Arcline serves as our personal electromagnetic force field preceding our aura, and nurturing it amplifies our personal power and attracts positivity into our life. By aligning our actions and words with both cosmic and human realms, it fosters clarity and certainty in our endeavors. However, neglecting it can lead to incongruence between our words and actions, resulting in a sense of disorientation and lack of focus.

Arcline at a Glance

- Purpose: Your Arcline helps your words and your actions match the intention, unique purpose, and potential of your higher self.
- In alignment: You act as the creator of your life, feel a strong connection through prayer, have mastery of word and action, in addition to experiencing high focus, concentration, and decisiveness. You are a strong manifester who is aligned with higher self and acts with integrity.
- Out of alignment: At the extreme, your work and actions are not consistent, your inner world does not match your outer world, and you have inner conflict, confusion, and feel victimized.
- Pose to practice: Archer pose
- Motto: I choose to create a life I love!

Body 7: Aura

Imagine the Aura as a shield of protection, an unseen yet potent force enveloping our being. Strengthening it is akin to donning cosmic armor against negativity. While life's challenges may still

THE YOGA OF SELF-AWARENESS   165

arise, with a fortified Aura, their impact is mitigated. Instead of being drained by drama, we radiate resilience, allowing us to serve others from a place of abundance rather than depletion.

AURA AT A GLANCE

- Purpose: By unveiling your purpose and radiating your brilliance from within to the world and protecting you against low vibes, it is your personal power suit for unleashing your inner badass.
- In alignment: You feel bright and uplifting, comfortable in your own skin, merciful and compassionate, magnetic, and are a pleasure to be around. Your shine comes from your inner core.
- Out of alignment: You feel lowered self-esteem and self-critical, and you may mock others who uplift and empower others. You feel disconnected from yourself and others, depressed, and have difficulty standing out.
- Pose to practice: Triangle pose
- Motto: I honor myself and uplift others as I go!

Body 8: Pranic Body

The core of Kundalini yoga's vitality is the Pranic Body. This aspect governs our breath and vital life force, offering a profound source of energy. When we overlook our Pranic Body, we may feel diminished and overshadowed by emotions like loneliness and fear. However, by harnessing our life force, a transformative shift occurs — we become connected, fearless, and embrace a life abundant with possibilities.

PRANIC BODY AT A GLANCE

- Purpose: It's the grand master of your life force — your prana — and your key to unparalleled energy and vitality.

- In alignment: You feel sustained energy, vibrant health, clear and creative, fearless, connected to the cosmos, confident, increased vitality, and spiritual awareness.
- Out of alignment: You experience loneliness, fearful thoughts, isolation, scarcity beliefs, fear of your dark side, low energy, poor health, and like you never have enough (money, love, time, and so on).
- Pose to practice: Bow pose
- Motto: My energy generates abundance in all areas of my life!

Body 9: Subtle Body

The Subtle Body serves as our cosmic conduit to the unseen and to our intuition. Nurturing it establishes a direct pathway to higher wisdom. When our Subtle Body flourishes, we seamlessly integrate this wisdom into our thoughts, shining brightly in our own brilliance. Yet neglecting our Subtle Body may leave us feeling disconnected from vital information, like playing a tune without all the instruments.

Remember: Real change often happens quietly, but it's incredibly impactful. When our Subtle Body is in sync, things just flow with style and grace, making us think, *Wow, that was easy.*

SUBTLE BODY AT A GLANCE

- Purpose: As the portal to higher insight and the unseen, its job is to seamlessly allow all-knowing wisdom to flow straight to you, unfiltered.
- In alignment: You have rock-solid intuition and insights, enhanced creativity, and a strong big-picture perception and inner knowing, and you feel one with your higher self, with unleashed potential.
- Out of alignment: You express anger and frustration;

information feels hidden; you feel misunderstood, undervalued, and skeptical of others; and you have difficulty
communicating effectively.
- Pose to practice: Alternating life nerve stretch
- Motto: I easily cocreate my reality with the cosmos!

Body 10: Radiant Body

The Radiant Body is our pathway to unlocking our individuality
and embracing our pure brilliance. It's more than just discovering
our inner star; it's about allowing our unique gifts, talents, and
strengths to radiate brightly like a guiding beacon. Nurturing our
Radiant Body opens doors to a life filled with boundless enthusiasm, unwavering self-assurance, and a magnetic charm. However,
failing to tend to it may leave our spirit feeling muted and con-
fined to a small space with limited growth.

Don't let fear hold you back; it's time to step onto the stage of
your dreams and shine. When you give life to your Radiant Body,
that's when you'll witness your full potential in all its glory. You
return to your radiance and shine brightly from the inside out.

RADIANT BODY AT A GLANCE

- Purpose: Its goal is to reveal your unique, fabulous self to
the world and give you permission to make a massive impact and be authentically, unapologetically YOU!
- In alignment: You feel unleashed uniqueness and self-
actualization — influencing others to do the same —
along with increased magnetism, more passion and joy,
and more courage and radiance.
- Out of alignment: You experience mundane goals, a lackluster work and lifestyle, fluctuating energy, a sense of
underachievement, and a disconnect from your gifts and
talents, and you settle for mediocrity.

- Pose to practice: Arm pumps
- Motto: I courageously express my uniqueness and unleash my full potential!

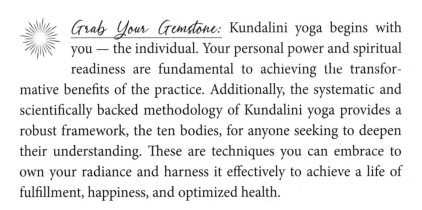 *Grab Your Gemstone:* Kundalini yoga begins with you — the individual. Your personal power and spiritual readiness are fundamental to achieving the transformative benefits of the practice. Additionally, the systematic and scientifically backed methodology of Kundalini yoga provides a robust framework, the ten bodies, for anyone seeking to deepen their understanding. These are techniques you can embrace to own your radiance and harness it effectively to achieve a life of fulfillment, happiness, and optimized health.

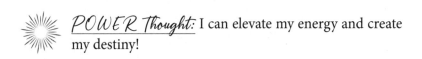 *POWER Thought:* I can elevate my energy and create my destiny!

POWER Up Your Practice 16: Poses for the Ten Bodies

Here are poses for each of the ten bodies. Use these to tap into the essence of each specific body and help you return to radiance.

Remember, you can download all this book's exercises in the complimentary Return to Radiance Personal Transformation Guide at Resources.ReturnToRadianceBook.com.

Soul Body: Lotus Pose

This classic seated posture with legs crossed and feet on top of thighs is used in meditation and breathing exercises. This pose is highly regarded for its ability to increase circulation in the lumbar spine, nourish the pelvic organs, and importantly, stabilize the mind and body to enhance the deeper aspects of meditation.

- Sit on the floor or a mat with your legs stretched out in front of you, spine erect.
- Bend your right knee, and use your hands to help place your right foot on your left thigh, ensuring that the sole faces upward and the heel is close to the abdomen. Repeat with the other leg, placing the left foot on your right thigh, with the sole facing upward.
- Half lotus is when the right foot rests on the left thigh, while the left foot rests beneath the right thigh. Easy pose is a simple cross-legged position, with both feet under the thighs. Use whichever version is most comfortable for you.
- Place your hands face up on your knees in a relaxed Gyan Mudra position, with index finger and thumb touching.
- Sit with your spine straight and your head aligned with your body. Close your eyes to enhance internal awareness.
- Hold this position and meditate for anywhere from three to eleven minutes. As you do, breathe deeply and focus on your breath. If you wish, focus on your intention to connect with your Soul Body. A common meditation is to visualize a light at the heart center that grows brighter with each breath, symbolizing the soul's purity and eternal nature.

Negative Mind: Bear Grip

Bear grip is used to create tension and release in the upper body, particularly focusing on the heart center. This pose is excellent for developing courage and clear decision-making, key aspects of a well-functioning Negative Mind.

- Sit in easy pose (cross-legged) with a straight spine. If sitting on the floor is uncomfortable, sit on a chair with your feet flat on the ground.
- To form bear grip, extend both arms straight out in front of your chest, parallel to the floor. Clench your right hand into a fist and wrap your left hand around it, palms facing each

other. Pull both arms away from each other, in opposite directions, without releasing the grip, creating tension across your chest and upper arms.

- For one to three minutes (gradually increasing duration with practice), alternate tensing and releasing, coordinating this with the breath. First, inhale deeply through the nose, hold the breath, and pull the arms apart with maximum tension. Then exhale forcefully through the mouth and relax the arms, but maintain the grip with your hands.
- To enhance concentration, focus your eyes on the tip of the nose.
- When finished, release the grip and gently shake out your hands and arms. Sit quietly for a few moments to integrate the effects of the exercise.

Positive Mind: Stretch Pose

Stretch pose is known for its ability to stimulate and strengthen the navel center, which in Kundalini yoga is closely tied to willpower and the ability to manifest positivity and assertiveness in life.

- Lie flat on your back on a yoga mat or comfortable surface, legs straight and arms parallel along your body, palms facing down.
- Keeping your legs straight, raise your head and heels about six inches off the ground. Look at your toes to keep your neck in alignment. This position ensures your lower back remains on the ground by engaging your core.
- For more challenge and to intensify the navel center activation, you can start by placing your hands under your buttocks to support your lower back.
- While holding this position for one to three minutes, use Breath of Fire (page 113), a rapid, rhythmic breath through the nose.

Neutral Mind: Easy Pose with Gyan Mudra and Sodarshan Chakra Kriya

Easy pose, or sitting cross-legged, is an ideal position for meditation and breathwork. Gyan Mudra, where the index finger and thumb touch, stimulates knowledge and ability. Combined with Sodarshan Chakra Kriya, which is one of the most powerful kriyas (or sequences) in Kundalini yoga, this provides profound support for the Neutral Mind.

- Sit in easy pose, with spine straight and shoulders relaxed.
- Place the backs of your hands on your knees in Gyan Mudra: Touch the tips of the index fingers to the tips of the thumbs, with the other fingers straight but relaxed.
- Next perform the Sodarshan Chakra Kriya: Close your eyes and focus on the brow point. Raise your right hand and block your right nostril with your right thumb. Inhale deeply through the left nostril. While holding the breath, silently repeat the mantra "Wahe Guru" four times as you pump your navel point three times for each mantra (for a total of twelve pumps). Release the right nostril, close the left nostril with your right little finger, and exhale slowly and completely through the right nostril.
- This completes one round. The next round starts by inhaling through the left nostril again. Do as many rounds as you wish, but aim to continue for three to eleven minutes. The full expression is sixteen rounds, while increasing the number of pumps during each mantra to twelve (or forty-eight pumps per round); work up to this.

Physical Body: Frog Pose

Frog pose is an excellent exercise for increasing lower-body flexibility, strengthening the legs, enhancing cardiovascular health, and stimulating the energy flow throughout the body. It is particularly good for activating the lower chakras, which relate to our physical existence.

- Stand straight with your heels together, toes turned out, and heels lifted off the ground, balancing on the balls of your feet. Bend your knees deeply, bringing your buttocks down toward your heels while keeping your heels elevated.
- Place your fingertips on the ground between your legs for balance, shoulders aligned over your hands.
- Coordinate the following movement with your breath: As you inhale, straighten your legs, lift your hips high, and keep your fingertips on the floor. Your head lowers toward the knees, and heels remain lifted. As you exhale, lower back down into the squat position, head up, chest open. Maintain focus on the breath and the movement.
- Continue this movement rhythmically and at a steady pace to maximize cardiovascular benefits. Start with twenty-six repetitions and gradually build up to over a hundred for a more intense practice.

Arcline: Archer Pose

Archer pose is a powerful pose that activates the Arcline, which enhances your radiance, confidence, and clarity of purpose. It's particularly useful for improving focus and willpower.

- Stand straight with your legs about two feet apart.
- Point your right foot forward and place your left foot at a forty-five-degree angle. Keep your left leg strong and bend your right knee till your right thigh is parallel to the ground; keep your right knee directly over your right ankle.
- Curl your fingers into your palms with your thumbs pointing upward. As if you are holding a bow and arrow, raise both arms to shoulder height, with the right arm straight ahead over the right leg and the left arm bent back as if pulling on the string. Keep the hands curled into fists with the thumbs pointing up.
- Fix your gaze past your right thumb, envisioning a target in

the distance. This enhances your focus and determination, key aspects of the Negative Mind's ability to discern effectively.

- Hold the pose while taking deep, steady breaths for one to three minutes, then switch sides and repeat.

Aura: Triangle Pose

Triangle pose is a standing yoga pose that opens up the lungs, works the legs, and stretches the muscles of the torso while increasing both physical and energetic stability and breadth — which is helpful for expanding and fortifying the Aura.

- Stand straight with your feet together. Step or jump your feet about three to four feet apart. Raise your arms to shoulder height, extending them front and back, palms facing down. Turn your right foot forward 90 degrees and turn your left foot slightly inward.
- Bend your torso to the right directly over the right leg, bending from the hip joint, not the waist. Reach forward as far as you can, then reach down with your right hand and allow it to rest against your right leg, wherever it falls naturally, while your left arm extends directly upward.
- Keep both legs straight, but it's OK to bend your knees slightly, so they aren't locked. Tighten your core to support your upper body. Turn your gaze upward at your raised left hand. If this is uncomfortable for your neck, look straight ahead. Ensure your body is bent sideways, not forward or backward; form a straight line that extends through the sides of your waist.
- While breathing deeply, hold the pose for up to a minute. When you're ready to come up, inhale and reach up through the left arm, lifting your torso upright, while pressing your back foot firmly into the floor. Repeat on the opposite side.

Pranic Body: Bow Pose

Bow pose is a back bend that stretches and strengthens the entire back of the body, while opening up the chest and lungs. This pose helps to improve the flexibility of the spine, increases internal organ function, and invigorates the Pranic Body by enhancing respiratory capacity.

- Lie on your stomach on a yoga mat with your legs stretched out behind you, hip-width apart, and your arms by the sides of your body.
- Bend your knees and reach back to take hold of your ankles or feet. Make sure to keep your knees hip-width apart throughout the pose to protect your lower back.
- Inhale and lift your heels away from your buttocks while also lifting your thighs off the mat. This action will naturally pull your upper torso and head off the mat.
- Draw your shoulders back and look forward. Keep your gaze forward and neck long to ensure you don't strain your neck.
- At first, hold the pose for only twenty or thirty seconds, but extend the time as your strength and flexibility improve. Throughout, breathe deeply and steadily, focusing on expanding your chest and ribs with each inhale to increase the capacity of your lungs.
- When finished, exhale and gently release your legs and chest to the mat. Lie face down and shake your hips from side to side to release any tension in the lower back.

Subtle Body: Alternating Life Nerve Stretch

The alternating life nerve stretch involves stretching the hamstrings and stimulating the sciatic nerve, enhancing flexibility and energetic flow. This pose particularly supports the Subtle Body by opening up the flow of energy through the energy channels and helping to refine sensory perceptions.

- Sit on the floor with your legs extended straight in front of you.
- Bend your left knee and bring the sole of your left foot to the inside of your right thigh, keeping your right leg straight. Inhale deeply as you raise your arms overhead, lengthening your spine.
- Exhale and slowly hinge forward from your hips, reaching toward the toes of your right foot with both hands. If you can reach your foot, gently pull on it to deepen the stretch; if not, just reach as far as comfortable. Hold the stretch for one to three minutes, breathing deeply and steadily. Focus on releasing tension in the back and hamstrings and feeling the flow of energy through the spine.
- Switch sides and stretch over the left leg. When you're finished, sit in easy pose and take a few deep breaths, allowing the energy to settle and integrate.

Radiant Body: Arm Pumps

Arm pumps synchronize vigorous arm movements with powerful breathing. This exercise stimulates the entire energy system, enhances stamina, and builds a magnetic and protective aura around the body.

- Sit in easy pose or in a chair, feet flat on the ground, and your spine straight.
- Extend both arms straight out in front of you, parallel to the ground, palms facing down.
- Begin pumping both arms together rapidly. As you do, lift both arms to the level of the shoulders and then bring them both down to the level of your navel. The movement is quick and powerful, about one full pump per second.
- Coordinate your breath with your arm movements. Inhale as you lift your arms and exhale as they lower. Use a strong, forceful breath to match the vigorous movement. Continue

for one to three minutes, and as you build stamina, increase to seven minutes or longer for a more profound effect.

- When finished, inhale deeply, raise your arms up above your head, and hold your breath for a few seconds while stretching the spine upward. Exhale and slowly lower your arms, then relax your breath and feel the energy circulating through your Aura.

CHAPTER SEVENTEEN

Engage the Energy Centers

*I*magine being able to promote and harness your own well-being and personal growth by tuning further inward. When you know yourself intimately on the inside, you become an unstoppable force on the outside. How handy would it be to tune in to yourself to elevate your energy, improve your well-being, and increase the flow of abundance in your life?

Your radiance is one part you, one part your soul, and one part Infinite Intelligence. This means we are two parts cosmic energy. We have an energy system inside us that is made up of chakras and meridians. These energy points are commonly referred to in acupuncture, yoga, and meditation, and they are a focal point in Kundalini yoga. This chapter focuses on the primary energy centers known as chakras, which represent different areas of life.

Recognizing the interconnectedness between your body, mind, and spirit deepens your connection with yourself, others, and the Universe. It fosters a greater sense of belonging and purpose, which then ignites more passion and fulfillment. Life is meant to be filled with meaning, joy, and celebration. As a society, we have spent way too long denying our soul's evolution. This has led to so much disease and despair. You have an opportunity to take your power back and get to know your energy intimately so you can not only thrive but fly.

Look at All Those Chakras

Sometimes, when we've done the mental, emotional, and physical work but still don't see the changes we desire, it might be our energy centers that need a reboot. That's where focusing on our chakras comes in. Activating and balancing them can give us the ultimate mind, body, and soul tune-up to operate at our peak potential. For instance, wearing their associated color or gemstone can give you a boost with their positive qualities. With these cosmic energy centers as your companions, you can rock that beautiful radiance of yours in new and magical ways.

Teachings on chakras have been around for thousands of years, going back to some of the oldest texts of Hindu philosophy. The word *chakra* means "wheel" in Sanskrit, and it refers to the spinning energy centers that exist within the human body.

The chakras are often depicted as spinning wheels of light located at different points along the central axis of the body, from the base of the spine to the crown of the head. Seven main chakras are described in most modern-day teachings, and I also describe the eighth chakra, known as the radiant chakra.

ENERGY CENTER 1: ROOT CHAKRA

- Theme: security and safety
- Location: base of spine
- Color: red
- Gemstone: red jasper

ENERGY CENTER 2: SACRAL CHAKRA

- Theme: emotional regulation and creativity
- Location: lower abdomen
- Color: orange
- Gemstone: carnelian

ENERGY CENTER 3: SOLAR PLEXUS CHAKRA

- Theme: courage and self-esteem
- Location: upper abdomen
- Color: yellow
- Gemstone: citrine

ENERGY CENTER 4: HEART CHAKRA

- Theme: love, wholeness, and belonging
- Location: heart
- Color: pink or green
- Gemstone: rose quartz

ENERGY CENTER 5: THROAT CHAKRA

- Theme: self-expression and truth
- Location: throat
- Color: turquoise
- Gemstone: turquoise

ENERGY CENTER 6: THIRD-EYE CHAKRA

- Theme: intuition and trust
- Location: center brow point (third eye)
- Color: indigo
- Gemstone: lapis lazuli

ENERGY CENTER 7: CROWN CHAKRA

- Theme: cosmic connection and divine guidance
- Location: top of head (crown)
- Color: purple
- Gemstone: amethyst

ENERGY CENTER 8: RADIANT CHAKRA

- Theme: oneness and self-actualization
- Location: aura
- Color: clear or golden
- Gemstone: clear quartz

Understanding the concept of chakras and their significance will deepen your awareness of your radiance. By aligning with the inherent wisdom of the body and tapping into its natural healing abilities, you will cultivate a sense of personal empowerment and agency in your life by engaging your energy centers.

Practical Mojo

Exploring techniques to activate and harmonize the chakras can promote holistic healing on physical, emotional, and spiritual levels. By addressing imbalances or blockages in specific energy centers, you will experience improved vitality, emotional resilience, and spiritual growth. Feeling jittery or ungrounded? It might be time to focus on grounding your root chakra. Need to express yourself authentically? The throat chakra might be calling for attention. Even though they are part of our cosmic DNA, they can be used very practically in our everyday life.

Our physical and emotional well-being is closely connected to the health of our energy centers, so cultivating self-awareness is essential. Practices like mindfulness, meditation, yoga, and energy healing can help you tap into the power of your chakras, enhancing your overall health, prosperity, and happiness.

These energy centers elevate your vitality, so integrate their cosmic energy into your daily routine. As you explore these powerful centers, pay attention to what resonates with you. Notice what feels balanced, what feels off, and where you may need some extra support. This awareness will serve as your guide to effectively incorporating these cosmic powerhouses into your everyday life.

Energy Center 1: Root Chakra

The root chakra serves as our foundational source of energy, emphasizing security, stability, and primal survival instincts.

When the root chakra becomes imbalanced, it can feel like facing off against those formidable foes anxiety and fear. These adversaries thrive on survival concerns, leading to feelings of instability and disconnection from reality. Physical symptoms like lower-back pain, digestive issues, or increased stress levels may manifest as a result of the imbalance.

When this chakra is balanced, you embody a sense of security and trust in life's flow, remaining grounded and resilient in the face of challenges. You excel at meeting your basic needs, and you confidently showcase your talents and strengths.

- Practical tip: Ground yourself in daily routines and rituals, such as a morning walk or meditation, to establish stability. This fosters a sense of security within and provides a foundation for emotional and mental well-being.
- Affirmation: I am safe and secure.

Energy Center 2: Sacral Chakra

The sacral chakra is the second vital energy center, focusing on creativity, emotions, and interpersonal connections. When this chakra falls out of alignment, mood swings become the norm, emotions feel stifled, and our once-vibrant creative spark dims. Relationships become complex, and our sense of self-worth retreats into the shadows.

When balanced, the sacral chakra ignites your creative prowess, enhances emotional intelligence, and infuses your life with vitality. Your relationships thrive, joy becomes a constant companion, and adaptability becomes second nature. This chakra serves as your gateway to expressing your unique gifts and talents, unlocking your inner brilliance.

- Practical tip: Engage in creative activities or hobbies regularly to unleash passion and joy. This enhances emotional balance and creativity, positively impacting mental health and overall satisfaction.
- Affirmation: I am joyful and creative.

Energy Center 3: Solar Plexus Chakra

The solar plexus chakra is the third vital energy center, focusing on personal power, self-esteem, and confidence. When this chakra falls out of alignment, self-doubt creeps in, confidence wanes, and decision-making becomes difficult. Our assertiveness either diminishes or becomes overly aggressive, and digestive issues are common. Suddenly, our super big dreamy goals seem elusive and too hard to go after.

When in harmony, you radiate with confidence and personal power, making decision-making effortless, and your self-esteem soars. Assertiveness becomes second nature, striking a balance between strength and humility, while motivation drives you toward your loftiest aspirations.

- Practical tip: Set and pursue achievable goals, breaking them down into manageable tasks. This boosts self-confidence and empowerment, influencing mental resilience and success in professional endeavors.
- Affirmation: I am strong and I am bold.

Energy Center 4: Heart Chakra

The heart chakra, the fourth energy center, is about love, compassion, and wholeness. When this chakra is out of balance, it's hard to navigate intimate relationships, whether romantic or family. Connecting with others becomes challenging, and we become very empathic, absorbing everyone's emotions. Feelings of loneliness and bitterness may seep in, accompanied by an inner critic. When dis-ease sets in, it's typically around the lungs and heart.

When aligned, your heart becomes open to love, exuding warmth and compassion toward yourself and others. Relationships flow effortlessly, fueled by empathy, and emotional capacity is expanded and feelings of joy and bliss emerge. Self-love is high as you embrace your inherent worthiness and wholeness.

- Practical tip: Practice gratitude and engage in acts of kindness to foster compassion. This enhances emotional intelligence, strengthens relationships, and positively impacts mental and emotional health.
- Affirmation: I am love and I am loved.
- Bonus affirmation: I am enough.

Energy Center 5: Throat Chakra

The throat chakra, our fifth energy center, revolves around speaking truth, self-expression, and creativity. When this chakra falls out of alignment, expressing thoughts feels burdensome, plagued by misunderstandings and communication breakdowns. Our voice, both literal and metaphorical, feels stifled, leading to inadvertent gossip or regrettable remarks. It becomes very hard to speak and communicate our truth. We might even find ourselves losing our voice.

When balanced, you effortlessly articulate thoughts with clarity and precision. Self-expression is second nature, whether through art, language, or any chosen medium. Most importantly, you possess the courage to voice your opinions, fostering relationships built on transparency and openness. You may even find yourself in roles or situations where you are using your voice as your medium of self-expression, be it singing, speaking, leading meetings, comedy, and so on.

- Practical tip: Express yourself authentically, whether through speaking, writing, or creative outlets. This promotes clear communication, which positively influences mental clarity and fosters meaningful connections.
- Affirmation: I speak my truth with clarity.

Energy Center 6: Third-Eye Chakra

The sixth energy center is known as the third-eye chakra. It is the epicenter of intuition, insight, and perception. When this chakra falls out of alignment, clarity and insight vanish, leaving us feeling uncertain. It's hard to connect to our intuition, which is our inner guidance system. Confusion and mental fog become constant, and headaches serve as our brain's protest against internal chaos.

When functioning optimally, your intuition is like your personal GPS, guiding you with unparalleled clarity. Your intuition becomes finely tuned, offering deep insights and strong instincts that make trusting your gut second nature. You emerge as a visionary, navigating your path with unwavering focus. You may find yourself in roles where you are guiding others because of your clarity and foresight.

- Practical tip: Incorporate mindfulness practices, like meditation, to enhance intuition. It improves mental focus, intuition, and decision-making, positively impacting overall mental and emotional well-being.
- Affirmation: I trust my intuition.

Energy Center 7: Crown Chakra

The crown chakra, the seventh energy center, is the pinnacle of spirituality, oneness, and enlightenment. When this chakra falls out of alignment, we feel very disconnected from life and as if life has no meaning. The Universe calls, yet we find ourselves missing the signs and signals. It's as if we can no longer experience them. Skepticism and cynicism regarding spiritual matters can obscure the path to self-actualization. Deep depression is a common trait of an out-of-alignment crown chakra.

When harmonized, you feel a profound sense of fulfillment. Inner peace flows effortlessly. Your awareness becomes multi-dimensional and revelations arrive with remarkable frequency. Your connection to your higher self deepens, forging a bond to a cosmic companionship, offering direct access to inspiration and purpose. You may find yourself aligning to more meaningful work that inspires and uplifts others.

- Practical tip: Connect with nature and engage in activities that foster a sense of spiritual connection. This nurtures a sense of purpose and connection to something greater, positively influencing mental and emotional resilience.
- Affirmation: I am one with the Universe and the Universe is one with me.

Energy Center 8: Radiant Chakra

The radiant chakra, also known as the soul star, represents the eighth energy center, emphasizing a deeper spiritual connection and alignment with our soul's purpose. When this chakra falls out of harmony, we might find ourselves searching for our purpose rather than having a deep understanding of it. Our spiritual guidance system is having a hard time connecting with us, leaving us feeling adrift, unsure of which direction to take. When this chakra is severely out of alignment, coping with life is extremely hard and we may numb ourselves through alcohol, drugs, work, food, and so on.

When attuned, you embody an awareness of higher self and walk in a confident stride along the path of your purpose and potential. Wrapped in a comforting embrace of divine love and compassion, this is where your unique gifts, talents, and strengths shine brightly, taking center stage in the grand theater of existence. You may find yourself in the role of teacher, whether that's a leadership role, a writer, a musician, a speaker, a podcaster, and so on. Sharing a message of hope, peace, happiness, and potential becomes a natural part of who you are. You deliver this in the uniqueness of your gifts, talents, and strengths.

- Practical tip: Practice self-reflection and connect with your inner self through activities like meditation and journaling. This strengthens the connection with your higher self, contributing to mental clarity, emotional balance, and spiritual growth.
- Affirmation: I am aligned with the highest truth and embrace my soul's infinite potential.

Tune In and Turn On

Engaging with the energy centers provides an opportunity for self-reflection and personal growth. By exploring the qualities associated with each chakra and how they manifest in life, you can gain insights into areas for development and transformation. Learning to activate and balance the energy centers empowers you to take an active role in your own healing and personal development journey. This will lead to establishing a holistic self-care routine that supports your overall well-being and spiritual growth.

Engaging your energy centers nurtures and balances the body's energy systems to promote holistic wellness, self-awareness, and personal transformation. Through intentional practice and exploration of the chakras, you can cultivate a deeper connection to yourself and the world around you, leading to greater vitality, harmony, fulfillment, and radiance.

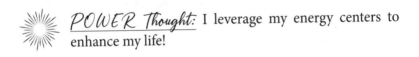

Grab Your Gemstone: As you integrate practices for these energy centers into your daily routine, you will harness their transformative power — elevating your vitality, prosperity, and happiness in every facet of life. Embrace this chakra journey of self-discovery, for within it lies the radiant brilliance of your true self, which is awaiting activation and alignment with the cosmic flow of your energy centers.

POWER Thought: I leverage my energy centers to enhance my life!

POWER Up Your Practice 17: Chakra Balancer

This fun and engaging exercise helps you experiment with your chakras, using a combination of visualization, movement, and affirmation to activate and balance each one. This exercise helps you explore your chakras and interact with them. The goal of this balancer is to help you activate and harmonize all eight energy centers through targeted movements, visualizations, and affirmations.

Do all eight chakras in one session, and recite each affirmation at least five times before moving on to the next. Take long deep breaths as you go.

- Root chakra: Stand firmly on the ground, feet shoulder-width apart. Slightly bend your knees. Visualize a red light at the base of your spine and mentally affirm, "I am safe and secure." As you repeat the affirmation, perform a few gentle squats while maintaining your focus on the base of your spine.
- Sacral chakra: Sit on the ground, legs extended forward. Lean back on your hands, bend your knees, and place the soles of your feet on the floor. Gently sway your knees from side to side. Imagine an orange glow in your lower abdomen and repeat, "I am joyful and creative."

- Solar plexus chakra: Stand or sit with your back straight. Place your hands on your stomach and take deep, powerful breaths. Visualize a yellow light spinning in your solar plexus and affirm, "I am strong and I am bold."
- Heart chakra: Sit cross-legged or in a chair. Place your hands on your chest. Breathe deeply and visualize a green or pink light radiating from your heart. As you breathe in, imagine love flowing into you, and as you breathe out, imagine love flowing out. Affirm, "I am love and I am loved."
- Throat chakra: Sit comfortably with a straight spine. Gently tilt your head back and forth, loosening the neck, and then straighten your neck and spine. Visualize a turquoise light at your throat, and chant or whisper, "I speak my truth with clarity."
- Third-eye chakra: Sit quietly with your eyes closed. Place your index finger on your third eye. Gently apply pressure, then release. Focus on the spot and visualize an indigo light, affirming, "I trust my intuition."
- Crown chakra: Sit or lie down in a relaxed position. Imagine a violet or white light flowing from the top of your head, connecting you to the Universe. Affirm, "I am one with the Universe, and the Universe is one with me."
- Radiant chakra: Sit or lie down in a comfortable position. Visualize a brilliant light above your head, expanding and glowing white. Affirm, "I am aligned with the highest truth and embrace my soul's infinite potential."

After moving through all the chakras, spend a few minutes in quiet reflection or meditation. Feel the energy flow through your body and visualize your entire being radiating with balanced, vibrant energy. Next, journal about your experience. What did you feel during each exercise? Did certain chakras feel more active or blocked than others? Did you experience anything else notable?

CHAPTER EIGHTEEN

Breath Becomes You

*D*id you know that the average adult breathes twenty thousand times a day? That's a lot of breathing! Breathing is something we do unconsciously every second of every day. The very fact that we are breathing means we are alive — but it doesn't mean we are living our best life. What if your breath could be conscious and purposeful? What if you could use it to increase your energy, reduce stress, improve stamina, access the answers within, and sparkle a little more? The good news is — you can! Your breath is the key to unlocking your vitality.

Breathwork is known to awaken dormant energy within the body, including kundalini energy — our primal power. Through intentional breathing practices, we can access heightened states of vitality, creativity, and spiritual awareness. Breathwork can also facilitate the release of stored emotions and traumas, allowing us to experience greater emotional freedom and resilience.

Our breath serves as a bridge between the physical body and the Universe, facilitating a deeper understanding of our true nature and connectedness to ourselves, others, and Infinite Intelligence. Each conscious inhale brings vitality and renewal, while each exhale offers surrender and release. Let's discover the transformative power of the breath.

Breathing Your Way Back to Radiance

The quality of your breath reflects the quality of your life. Most working adults have shallow unconscious breathing. Their focus is on their job, their responsibilities, their family, the bills, the overwhelm, and very seldomly on their breath. As a result, they live unconsciously. Every day seems to be on repeat with little variety; their relationships aren't fulfilling. Everything feels sadly shallow and lackluster. However, people who regularly practice intentional deep breathing, who consciously use breathwork, often have deep relationships and take intentional actions. Their life is consciously created and feels purposeful, just like their breath. Your breath becomes who you are.

I want to help you not only return to your radiance but live in your radiance. Your breath is the most powerful asset you have because without it there is no life force. Expressing reverence for this beautiful force can help you create a life of depth and meaning.

Your breath is a tool for transformation. In Kundalini yoga, the breath is revered as a potent vehicle for transformation and self-realization. Through specific breathing techniques, we can harness the innate power of the breath to awaken dormant energies, balance the mind and body, and elevate our consciousness to higher states. Each breath is an opportunity for profound inner expansion. By cultivating conscious awareness of the breath, you tap into the subtle energy currents flowing within and around you, aligning with Universal life force energy.

The breath serves as a bridge between your physical body and the great big Universe, facilitating a deeper understanding of your true nature and interconnectedness with all beings. Through rhythmic and intentional breathing practices, you will be able to release energetic blockages, dissolve limiting beliefs, and access heightened states of clarity, creativity, and intuition.

Ultimately, the teachings of Kundalini yoga remind us that the breath is not merely a biological function but a sacred tool for inner alchemy and self-transcendence. Through dedicated practice and reverence for the breath, you can unleash your full potential and experience profound transformation in all areas of life.

Inhales and Exhales

Breathing techniques vary. Some inhale and exhale through the nose and some do so through the mouth. For the most part, resting breaths like long deep breathing use the nose. On your inhale, your abdomen and chest area are meant to rise. We breathe like this when we are babies, but as adults, our breath often becomes shallow, making it harder to tell at a glance if we are breathing correctly.

It's not uncommon for adults to pull their stomach and abdomen inward, rather than expand them outward, on the inhale. This happens when stress impacts the natural breathing rhythm. When you practice a few long and slow inhales through your nose, ensure your breath fills you up, expanding your abdomen and chest area outward.

For long deep breathing, exhale out the nose until you empty your breath. Pull your abdomen and chest area inward, toward your spine, on the exhale. As a variation, some techniques inhale through the nose and exhale through the mouth.

Layer mindfulness into your inhales and exhales, too. Set the intention that your breath connects to your personal power, to vitality and clarity. A long deep inhale can be used to reset yourself, and as you exhale, actively let go of stress and all that does not serve you.

Four Breathing Exercises to Increase Your Radiance

Here are four breathing techniques that are available to you anytime, anywhere. All will connect you to the limitless potential within and around you, as well as help you ground yourself deeper in your true essence.

Long Deep Breathing

Sit comfortably with a straight spine. Inhale deeply and slowly through the nose, allowing your abdomen and chest area to rise and expand fully. As you do, envision life force energy and infinite wisdom entering you. Exhale slowly and completely through the nose, drawing the abdomen in toward the spine until there is no breath left to exhale. As you do, consciously breathe out and release any stress and anxiety. Focus on making the inhales and exhales equal in duration.

Long deep breathing calms the mind, reduces stress, increases lung capacity, and oxygenates the blood.

Breath of Fire

Breath of Fire generates heat in the body, purifies the blood, strengthens the nervous system, and increases energy levels. It's excellent for detoxification and increasing vitality. This technique involves a short period of rapid, sharp breaths, in which you exhale fully while contracting your diaphragm and abdomen. For instructions, see POWER Up Your Practice 11: Breath of Fire with Root Lock (pages 113–15).

Alternate-Nostril Breathing

Sit comfortably with a straight spine. Close your right nostril with your right thumb and inhale deeply through the left nostril. Close the left nostril with your ring finger, release the right nostril, and exhale. Then inhale through the right nostril, close it with your right thumb, open your left nostril, and exhale. This completes one cycle. Continue alternate-nostril breathing for several rounds or for as long as you like.

Alternate-nostril breathing balances the flow of life force energy in the body, calms the mind, improves focus, and harmonizes the left and right hemispheres of the brain. It's deeply relaxing and centering.

Cooling Breath

Curl your tongue into a tube shape between your lips; if you can't curl your tongue, simply purse your lips. Inhale deeply through your tongue and open mouth, feeling the cool air entering. Close your mouth and exhale slowly through the nose. Continue for several rounds.

Cooling breath calms the body and mind, reduces excess heat, and soothes irritation. It's beneficial during hot weather or times of emotional intensity.

Practicing these four breathwork techniques will help reduce stress and anxiety and elevate your energy. They will also heighten your awareness and strengthen the connection between your mind, body, and soul. As you harness the transformative potential of your breath, you'll gain confidence in your ability to navigate life's challenges with greater ease and manifest your super big dreamy goals with more flow.

Grab Your Gemstone: Conscious breathing has transformative power. It elevates your vitality, reduces stress, and unlocks your inner potential. Breathwork is a means to awaken dormant energy, release emotional blockages, and deepen your connection with yourself and the Universe. Use it intentionally to get heightened states of clarity, creativity, and intuition, leading to a profound inner shift and expansion. Ultimately, your breath becomes who you are.

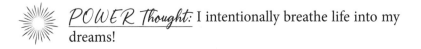 *POWER Thought:* I intentionally breathe life into my dreams!

POWER Up Your Practice 18:
Pick a Breath and Practice

This exercise is simple: Try all four of this chapter's breathing practices at least once. Then pick one and consciously use it up to three
times a day for a week. As you do, journal about your experience
and notice any improvements day to day and at the end of the
week. If you feel inspired, do a weeklong practice with each breath
for a month.

CHAPTER NINETEEN

Embrace the Magic of Mantra

Words have magic and power. Words carry energy. Just like our emotions have a radiant frequency and a frequency of UN-potential, so do our words.

The hidden power behind our words lies in their ability to shape our reality and influence our thoughts, emotions, and actions. Embracing mantra — that is, sacred sounds or phrases repeated during meditation or while chanting — can enhance our well-being and help us reach our potential.

Mantras carry ancient wisdom and spiritual energy, serving as a tool for transformation and manifestation. By repeating mantras with intention, you can align your consciousness with their inherent power, allowing it to penetrate your subconscious and reprogram limiting beliefs and patterns. The power of sound vibrations harmonizes your energy centers or chakras, balances your emotions, and quiets the mind. In group settings, the magic of mantra multiplies.

By repeating mantras, either silently or out loud, either by yourself or with others, you dissolve the illusion of separateness and awaken to the inherent oneness of all creation, fostering a sense of unity, love, and compassion. By harnessing the hidden power behind your words, and embracing mantra as a sacred practice, you can enhance your well-being, expand your consciousness, and unlock your highest potential.

Feeling the Magic

Mantras have been used for thousands of years. They have been embraced by many cultures as a way to connect to the divine and to expand consciousness. You may have experienced a mantra as a hymn in a religious setting, a chant in yoga class, or as affirmations in a personal growth workshop. If you have, remember the feeling as the group sang or chanted or shouted together in unison.

The first time I experienced the power of mantra was at a group session with Gabrielle Bernstein many years ago. The group was given a mantra to chant. After a few minutes, I could feel an unseen force fill the air. The more in sync we became, the more I could feel this energy intensify. Tears began rolling down many faces — we were being brought back to our radiance. By the end, something subtle yet magical connected us all. We rose above separateness, and for a brief time, we were all one. Mantra had shifted us back into our radiance and increased our sense of belonging both within that room and with humanity.

Mantras rewire our brains and connect us with Infinite Intelligence. From the moment we begin to utter their words, the way the tongue hits the upper palate sends signals to the brain that it's time to connect with our highest self. From affirmations to positive self-talk to intention-based mantras, our words shape our future.

If you have joined in group mantra, recall what the group energy felt like. Did you feel more connected to your higher self?

Embracing Mantra and Chanting

Our bodies are made up of energy. We're like tuning forks that respond to different frequencies. Mantras and chanting create powerful vibrations that resonate deeply within and offer transformation. When we chant or repeat mantras, those vibrations harmonize our physical, mental, and emotional states. It's like hitting the reset button and aligning ourselves with a higher frequency.

Their special sounds, words, and phrases, repeated silently or aloud, connect us to Infinite Intelligence and elevate our energy. Like so many of the practices in this book, they help reduce stress, anxiety, and depression, which keep us disconnected from our radiance and stuck in the zone of UN-potential. The more you can use practices like mantra, the more you take back control and choose to live in your radiance.

Mantras have the power to reprogram the mind. It's like hitting Ctrl/Alt/Delete on negative or limiting beliefs. By consciously choosing positive, uplifting phrases, you replace those old thought patterns with new, empowering ones. Their transformative power is a deeply personal journey, as the benefits vary from person to person. They range from relaxation and stress reduction to profound spiritual experiences and self-realization. It's an opportunity for personal growth, self-discovery, and inner transformation. So open your heart, open your mind, and embrace mantra as a tool to express your truest potential. Practicing mantra involves several steps, and the process can be tailored to individual preferences and beliefs.

- Choose a mantra: Select a word, phrase, or mantra-based music that holds personal significance or resonance for you. It could be a traditional Sanskrit mantra like "Om" or something high vibrational like "I am," or it could be any word or affirmation. The key is to choose something that feels meaningful and uplifting to you. I provide music-based mantras on my website at Resources.ReturnToRadianceBook.com.
- Find a comfortable posture: Sit in a comfortable position with your spine straight and shoulders relaxed. You can sit cross-legged on the floor, in a chair with your feet flat on the ground, or even lie down if that's more comfortable.
- Settle into stillness: Close your eyes gently and take a few

deep breaths to center yourself. Allow your body and mind to relax, releasing any tension or distractions.

- Begin repetition: Start repeating your chosen mantra, silently or aloud. You can synchronize the repetition with your breath, chanting the mantra on the inhale and the exhale, or you can simply repeat it at a steady pace. Focus your attention fully on the sound and vibration of the mantra.

- Maintain focus: As you repeat the mantra, be present with each repetition, letting go of any thoughts or distractions that arise. If your mind starts to wander, gently bring your focus back to the mantra without judgment.

- Practice regularly: Set aside dedicated time each day to practice mantra meditation. Start with a few minutes and gradually increase the duration as you become more comfortable with the practice. Consistency is key to experiencing the full benefits of mantra meditation.

- Reflect and integrate: After your meditation session, take a few moments to reflect on your experience. Notice any shifts in your thoughts, emotions, or state of mind. Consider how you can integrate the qualities of the mantra into your daily life.

By following these steps and cultivating a regular mantra meditation practice, you can tap into the transformative power of sound and vibration, promoting inner peace, clarity, and spiritual growth.

Grab Your Gemstone: Mantras, sacred sounds, or phrases repeated during meditation hold the key to unlocking your truest potential and returning you to your radiance. Through mantra repetition, you connect back to Universal energy, facilitating personal transformation and manifestation of your desires. Whether uttered alone or in a group, mantras serve as bridges between your physical self and the infinite cosmos, offering renewal, clarity, and connection.

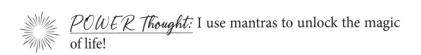 *POWER Thought:* I use mantras to unlock the magic of life!

POWER Up Your Practice 19: The Magic Mantra

I'm so excited to share this mantra with you because it is my absolute favorite meditation for vibrating with the cosmos. This is the Ek Ong Kar mantra I experienced at the Gabrielle Bernstein event, and now I have the pleasure of teaching it to you. It's known as the "magic mantra" for its ability to bring your deepest desires into manifestation.

The Ek Ong Kar mantra, a cornerstone in Kundalini yoga, holds immense transformational power. It embodies the very essence from which the entire Universe sprang. *Ek Ong Kar* translates to "One Creator created this Creation": *Ek* signifies the concept of "one"; *Ong* represents the divine consciousness infusing all existence; and *Kar* denotes creation or manifestation. The full mantra — Ek Ong Kar Sat Gur Prasad — is said to elevate us beyond duality and establish a cosmic connection so strong that we and the Universe become one, allowing spirit to harmoniously flow through us. I recommend doing this mantra for at least a week.

Chanting this mantra elevates your vibration, steadies the mind, and fosters a profound connection with the cosmic energy that surrounds you and dwells within. It most definitely returns you to your radiance.

Don't worry about chanting these unfamiliar words perfectly. It's more important to assume the intent and let the tongue hit the upper palate of the mouth. Your higher self will know what to do.

I also recommend chanting this to Ek Ong Kar mantra music. My favorite is Jai-Jagdeesh, "Expand into Intuitive Knowing." Find this on YouTube or a music streaming app, or see the resources on my website (Resources.ReturnToRadianceBook.com).

- Sit in a comfortable meditation posture, either cross-legged on the floor or on a chair with your feet flat on the ground. Hold your hands in Gyan Mudra (page 171) on top of your knees.
- Close your eyes and focus on your breath, allowing it to become slow, deep, and rhythmic. Inhale and exhale deeply, allowing yourself to get centered.
- If using Ek Ong Kar mantra music, start the music and begin chanting along with it. If chanting on your own, simply begin and maintain a gentle and consistent rhythm. Inhale and exhale in coordination with the chant. If using music, make sure your voice is audible. Allow the sound of your voice to resonate from your navel point; feel the vibration in this area. As you chant, let go of distractions and keep your mind focused on the sound and vibration of the mantra.
- Chant for at least eleven minutes, or longer if you prefer. When you're finished, take a deep breath in, hold briefly while applying Root Lock (page 115), and exhale. Then sit quietly for a few moments, allowing the effects of the meditation to settle within — and finish with a ginormous smile on your face!

CHAPTER TWENTY

Vibrate with the Cosmos

Some people imagine that meditation requires backpacking through mountains to sit with Tibetan monks. More often, people don't meditate because they think they are too busy or need the perfect quiet space. Meditation is funny like that. It's one of the hardest simple practices. Meditation doesn't care who we are or where we are. It exists to serve everyone — to elevate our energy and return us to radiance.

Meditation can seem complicated because there are so many traditions and ways to practice it. There are guided, silent, sound, mantra, and visualization meditations, and the list goes on! But meditating successfully requires just two things: doing it and having a high-frequency intention while you meditate. The rest is just the extras! Meditation can have an impact in as little as three minutes. Three minutes a day of quietude with a positive intention can totally transform you and your life.

My goal is to motivate and empower you to embrace meditation. Yes, meditation reduces stress and calms anxiety, but it also opens doors of opportunity. Each time we do it, it reveals a little more of the Universe's sparkle and shine. Through meditation, we can vibrate with the cosmos and open up new channels of consciousness and awareness that truly ignite our soul and unleash our potential.

Focus on Your Radiance

I learned a hard lesson that what we focus on when we meditate truly matters. It impacts our health and well-being directly, and our focus determines if that's for the better or for the worse. Be mindful of this as you explore meditation. We have all experienced stress, trauma, and drama — all the BS that holds us back. The things that have happened to you may have altered you from your radiance, but you don't need to dwell in that energy. You are not broken and there is nothing wrong with you. Yes, we need to acknowledge our pain and fears, we need to honor those feelings, but when we meditate, we need to acknowledge and honor our radiance.

I had just completed eighteen months of trauma-awareness and limited-beliefs certifications. During that time, meditations often focused on our personal trauma and stress. Even though the goal was to untangle from our trauma and live stress-free, the focus during meditation was still on the problem. At this point, I had already spent seven years as a Kundalini yoga teacher. I was familiar with meditation, and over that period, the intention of meditations was usually on my potential and on my radiance. That is, during meditation, I focused on the solution to the problems caused by trauma and stress.

Toward the end of the eighteen-month certification program, I noticed that many of my autoimmune symptoms had started to return, even though I was in remission. I couldn't figure out what was wrong, so I had my functional medicine practitioner order blood work. What we found was that my stress levels and inflammation levels were the highest they had been in two years. At first, I couldn't put my finger on what I was doing differently. Then it dawned on me. For nearly two years, my meditations had been focused on stress and trauma relief rather than on vibrating with the cosmos, like I used to do.

I decided to stop the stress- and trauma-based meditations

and return to my radiance- and potential-based meditations —
many of which I share in this book. The most miraculous thing
happened. Within a month, my autoimmune symptoms were
gone. Not only that but life was buzzing and humming again with
opportunities, and I had a sparkling mood to go along with it.

How meditation impacts us reflects what we put into it and
how we approach it. As in all things, our intentions make the
difference. Meditate intending to manifest your radiance and potential, even if it's just for three minutes a day, and you will see
your life shift in incredible and profound ways.

SET Yourself Free

Engaging in conscious breathing and meditation for just three
minutes daily opens the door to a trio of transformative wonders
often overlooked in our quest for fulfillment: space, energy, and
time. Beyond surface-level desires like financial success or achieving goals, high performers and leaders yearn for these deeper elements to enrich their lives.

- Space represents the freedom to breathe and be present.
- Energy embodies vitality beyond artificial stimulants.
- Time signifies the elusive resource needed to pursue pas-
  sions and dreams.

I like to refer to these desires by the acronym SET, and I encourage you to make the "SET yourself free promise" — which
is a pathway to reclaiming your radiant, gifted, and vibrant self,
all without spending a dime. This is simply pledging to practice
meditation regularly, which is the key to unlocking this promise,
revitalizing your spirit, and setting your soul free from the mo-
notony of living on autopilot. With regular meditation, the space
within blossoms with more passion, purpose, and a desire to just
be. With more space, your energy and vitality improve, which
increases the desire to pursue goals, dreams, and ambitions. As

a result, you spend time more effectively on more-meaningful pursuits. Conversely, neglecting meditation can have a steep cost, leaving us trapped in a cycle of repetition while the world brims with untapped experiences awaiting discovery.

Unlocking the wonders of Infinite Intelligence doesn't demand hours of meditation. As I say, even three-minute sessions can work wonders. It's like a quick shot of soul-boosting espresso amid the daily hustle. Even during chaotic weeks, you can carve out micro moments for meditation — I squeeze in mini-sessions even during crazy hectic workdays.

Meditation isn't about perfectionism, and we don't need a fancy cushion or a secluded cave. Anywhere, anytime, we can connect with the cosmos. If you're unsure where to begin, try any of the meditations or breathing practices in this book or choose to meditate to a song with spiritual resonance. Personally, Matisyahu's "One Day" was my gateway to meditation. It showed me there's no "right" way to meditate. No strict rules, no perfect environment — just you and your choice of practice. Savor that soul-boosting shot and let your limitless potential unfold.

Three Minutes for Your Soul

Be honest — you have three minutes a day that you could spare to meditate. We all do. That's all our souls need, a minimum of three minutes a day. You can meditate for longer and that would be great. You can explore different kinds of meditations beyond those in this book, and that would be fabulous. What isn't fabulous? When our souls don't get to vibrate with the cosmos for at least three minutes a day.

Here are instructions for an easy three-minute meditation:

- Find a quiet place — it can be anywhere, even a bathroom!
- Set the timer on your phone for three minutes.

- Set the intention for your radiance and your potential to manifest through you.
- Start the timer, close your eyes, and practice long deep breathing (page 192).
- If there is any background noise, allow it to become part of the experience.
- When thoughts arise, let them pass without controlling or judging them. If you get caught up in thoughts, say to yourself, *Three, two, one, begin again.* Use this quick little mantra to restart mental quietude as many times as needed.
- When the timer goes off, take a long deep inhale, hold it for two seconds, and then release a long deep exhale.

From everyday working professionals to stay-at-home parents to business moguls to famous artists and athletes, we all can vibrate with the cosmos — there are no exclusions. We all have the ability to return to our radiance and shine in the brilliance of our unique gifts, talents, and strengths.

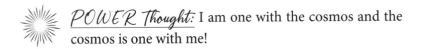 *Grab Your Gemstone:* Meditation is a simple yet profound tool that does not require perfect settings or extended periods of time to be effective. Incorporate meditation into your daily routine, even if only for three minutes, to enhance your radiance and unlock your potential. By setting high-frequency intentions during meditation, you can transform your life, open doors to new opportunities and experiences, and vibrate with the cosmos.

POWER Thought: I am one with the cosmos and the cosmos is one with me!

POWER Up Your Practice 20: Kirtan Kriya

Here is the neural-pathway-changing, pattern-breaking, life-elevating Kirtan Kriya meditation, also known as the Sa Ta Na Ma meditation. After doing this meditation daily for ninety days, it shattered my old stuck ways and catapulted me into a new stratosphere. You don't have to do this meditation for ninety days — but if you do, it will turbo-boost your personal transformation. This mantra meditation is well worth the eleven minutes it takes.

This is considered one of the most powerful mantra meditations for breaking habits and addictions. This includes negative self-talk. The magical combination of breathwork, mantra, mudra (purposeful movements with hands and fingers), and meditation break up those old troublesome patterns and create new powerful ones that support our evolution into greatness.

While everyone experiences something different, here are the typical benefits: It sharpens the mind and boosts focus, massively reduces stress and anxiety, fosters emotional regulation, banishes depression, rewires the brain for success, upgrades neural connections to optimize personal growth, enhances restful sleep and energized mornings, and fires up the intuition, helping us trust our gut and gain access to deeper insights. As you can see, there's a lot to this bad boy. So let's jump in!

To unlock the full power of Kirtan Kriya, consistent and regular practice is key. I recommend eleven minutes a day for forty days. If you wish to have a guided experience, do this mantra meditation along with Kirtan Kriya music; download online or go to Resources .ReturnToRadianceBook.com.

Sit in a comfortable cross-legged position on the floor or on a chair with your spine straight. Rest your hands on your knees with the palms facing upward.

The mantra is "Sa Ta Na Ma." Each syllable is pronounced with an open *a*, like "saw" or "ma." Here is what each syllable means:

- *Sa* means birth, the beginning of everything that was, is, or will be.
- *Ta* means life, existence, and creativity.
- *Na* means the ending of what was, transformation, and change.
- *Ma* means rebirth, regeneration, and resurrection.

As you chant the Kirtan Kriya mantra, also use the following mudra, or hand positions. Each hand position corresponds to a syllable. Here is the mudra sequence:

- While chanting "Sa," touch the tip of the thumb with the index finger — also known as the Jupiter finger, representing wisdom and knowledge.
- While chanting "Ta," touch the tip of the thumb with the middle finger — also known as the Saturn finger, representing patience and self-discipline.
- While chanting "Na," touch the tip of the thumb with the ring finger — also known as the Sun finger, representing vitality and personal power.
- While chanting "Ma," touch the tip of the thumb with the pinkie finger — also known as the Mercury finger, representing communication and intuition.

Chant for at least eleven minutes, repeating the mantra and the mudra. As you do, visualize each syllable of the mantra as the cosmic letter L flowing in from the Universe through the top of the head, moving down to the brow point (the spot between the eyebrows, or the third eye), then back out to the Universe through the brow point. Envisioning the L shape helps to strengthen the connection between the pineal gland, which plays a role in elevated levels of consciousness, and the pituitary gland, which plays a role in strengthening intuition. Together, they aid in your true self emerging and your potential being realized.

When you are finished, do a Root Lock (page 115). Inhale

deeply, hold the breath briefly, and squeeze up and in on your sex organs, your anus, and your lower region, then exhale.

Take a few moments to sit quietly and observe any sensations or effects in your body and mind, and journal your experience. Remember you are doing a most epic self-discovery experiment, so have fun with this and document your experience. It's really cool to look back on your thoughts even years later.

PART FIVE

ROCK YOUR
Radiance

Nothing can dim the light which shines from within.

— MAYA ANGELOU

CHAPTER TWENTY-ONE

The Knowing

*I*f you have ever known something to be true without being sure how you know it, that is the Knowing.

Everyone has it. It's invisible yet makes itself known, whether through gut feelings, hunches, or simply the certainty that something is true. The Knowing is the part of us that has no limits. It's the drop of the Universe that dwells freely within. It is an energy infused with Infinite Intelligence. When we have a relationship with it and understand its communication, it helps us rock our radiance.

Like my dad, the Knowing might express itself as a musical gift, the ability to effortlessly play an instrument. Like when I cleared up my autoimmune disease symptoms, the Knowing might guide you to the foods you need to heal or optimize your health. It can show up when you need to make an important decision, providing a clear yes or no.

This chapter explores how you can learn to tap into the Knowing and harness it as a trusted companion on your journey to return to radiance.

The Knowing in Action

The Knowing shows up in many ways — and it shows up differently for each person. That is because we are all unique and wired differently. Learning how to discern the various ways it shows up for you will help you rock your radiance on an ongoing basis. You are on your way to realizing the fullness of your potential, and strengthening your relationship with the Knowing will keep you moving forward.

Here are seven ways the Knowing communicates:

1. Gifts, strengths, talents: We all have something we are naturally good at or proficient in. This is the Knowing flowing through us. In doing the thing that you naturally know how to do well, you strengthen your relationship with the Knowing, enhancing your intuition and instincts.

2. Creative arts: Dancing, singing, writing, acting, painting, and any other creative activity is a form of the Knowing working through us. Somehow, you know what needs to be painted or written or sung. You don't know how you know but you know. It's second nature. The more you allow the Knowing to flow through you, the more fulfillment and joy it brings.

3. Recurring thoughts: Whenever a thought pops into our heads over and over again, there's a good chance it's the Knowing trying to get our attention. Whether it is a business idea or about a person, the more you can acknowledge recurring thoughts and explore their merit, the more the Knowing will show up and aid in your decision-making as well as overall confidence.

4. Body talk: The Knowing shows up to guide us to what is and what is not physically healthy for us. For example, shoulder pain is the Knowing telling us something isn't right and we need to pay attention to our environment. It could show up as increased energy after we do something good for us, such as going for a run or lying out in the sun. It communicates through our inner yes-and-no energy, and the more we listen the more likely we are to have good health.

5. Food insights: Food is another way in which the Knowing communicates. Have you ever eaten something and immediately gotten heartburn? That is the Knowing saying that food isn't vibing with you and you shouldn't eat it. Food also can be medicine and lead to healing and optimizing health. When digestion is easy and energy is produced, this is the Knowing saying, *Do more of this — your body likes this!*

6. Gut instincts: The Knowing shows up as our gut instincts, as visceral reactions, such as feeling sick to our stomach or getting butterflies and goose bumps. The more we tune in and listen to these reactions, the more they work in our favor and help us navigate life with more joy and ease.

7. Dreams and signs: Dreams, daydreams, and signs are other common ways the Knowing shows up. Have you ever had a dream that came true in real life? Or asked for a sign from the Universe, and then shortly thereafter the Universe responded with one? This is the Knowing. It can also show itself in daydreams or flights of imagination like a short movie clip. This is the Knowing trying to communicate on a visual level. Acknowledge and trust these experiences, which increases trust and faith in yourself and boosts your unstoppable spirit.

In a journal, make a list of experiences that reflect times the Knowing has tried to communicate with you. In what ways have you experienced it? Explore further the ones that resonate most with you. How has the Knowing helped serve you in the past?

Engage the Knowing Day to Day

Learning to work with the Knowing daily will help connect you to the truth of who you are as well as keep you on the path of truest potential. Its goal is to support you and help you shine. It wants you connected to your radiance and to your unique self-expression — unapologetically. Here are ways you can strengthen your relationship with the Knowing and engage with it in your day-to-day life.

- Acknowledge it: Acknowledging that the Knowing is part of you and making it an active part of your life is an important aspect of the reclaiming process. For many, the Knowing has been ignored or dismissed, so reinforcing that you regard it as a trusted companion will increase its presence as a daily ally.

- Ask it for help: The Knowing is an interactive part of your spirit, so you can talk to it and ask it for help. Whether you talk to it in your head or out loud doesn't matter. Simply speak to the all-knowing part of yourself directly: "Hello, Knowing, I need your help today. I have a really busy day at work, and I will need some help navigating today and making good decisions. Please help me clarify the right decisions." Or say: "Hello, Knowing, I'm really trying to understand what foods and exercises are good for me. Can you help me by making the answers easy for me to understand?" Once you have given it permission to work with you on a deeper level, the Knowing will be jumping for joy.

- Listen to its whispers: The Knowing is always communicating with us. Get still a couple times a day so that you can listen to its whispers. We often move at such a rapid pace that we become disconnected from the Knowing, our radiance, and our overall sense of self. Listening to its whispers helps to guide you down your best path and helps you stay connected to yourself, others, and the Universe. Every day, find an opportunity to get still and listen.

- Have fun and laugh: When we are having fun and laughing, we release tension and the blocks that keep us separated from the Knowing. Chronic stress and anxiety make it hard to hear the communication from the Knowing, the infinite part of ourselves. Enjoyment opens up those channels and invites the Knowing to be a cocreator in your life, helping to bring your dreams into realization. Find opportunities every day to sprinkle in a little fun.

Sharpen Your Focus with Your RAS

In addition to the daily ways you can interact with the Knowing, the reticular activating system (RAS) is another tool at your disposal.

The RAS is like a traffic controller in our brains, managing the flow of information to keep us alert and focused. It's responsible for regulating our sleep-wake cycle, determining what we pay attention to, and maintaining our overall level of alertness. Think of it as a filter, sifting through the constant stream of sensory input to highlight what's important so we can safely ignore the rest. Without the RAS, our brains would be overwhelmed by stimuli, making it difficult to function effectively in daily life.

Imagine that you just got a brand-new red Corvette. You are excited because you feel it's so unique, and then all of a sudden you start seeing red Corvettes everywhere. You might even think to yourself, *Is this a new thing or have there always been this many red Corvettes?*

Has something similar ever happened to you? This is your RAS filtering what it thinks is important to you. Its job is to sharpen your focus, so why not use it intentionally?

When you engage your RAS with intention, not only does your brain do what it is supposed to do, but the human side of you — your RAS — and the infinite side of you — the Knowing — partner up. They get in cahoots with each other to bring you the very thing that you are seeking, especially when it's in your highest and greatest good.

This is why things like vision boards and clearly defined goals work so well in helping us manifest our desires into reality. Together, our brain and the Universe bring it into reality. Yes, the limitless part of ourselves is conspiring in our favor, and our brains are sorting things out and making sure whatever we deem to be important gets filtered up to our awareness.

Here are a few ways in which to engage the RAS:

- Set clear goals: Clearly define your goals and aspirations. When you have a specific target in mind, your RAS is more likely to prioritize information relevant to those goals and filter out distractions.
- Visualize success: Visualize yourself achieving your goals in vivid detail. By consistently visualizing success, you prime your RAS to recognize opportunities and resources that align with your vision.
- Use affirmations: Practice affirmations that name your abilities, strengths, and desired outcomes. Positive affirmations help program your RAS to focus on opportunities that support your aspirations.
- Create vision boards: Create a vision board or collage that represents your goals and dreams. Displaying visual reminders of your aspirations can keep them at the forefront of your mind, prompting your RAS to seek out opportunities related to your vision.

The more you engage your RAS, the more you engage the Knowing to work for you and support you. Your radiance is all about expressing the fullness of who you are and what you can be. Embrace the Knowing and your life will unfold in the most beautiful ways.

 Grab Your Gemstone: The Knowing is there to guide you and support you in making decisions with more clarity and confidence. It also helps bring your dreams and goals into existence, both through Infinite Intelligence and leveraging the reticular activating system. Merging the mystical and the practical will support you in realizing the fullness of your potential and shining bright in your radiance.

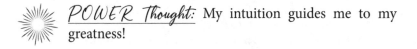 *POWER Thought:* My intuition guides me to my greatness!

POWER Up Your Practice 21: Make a Vision Board

Creating a vision board is a powerful tool for aligning your intentions with the Universe and leveraging the RAS to manifest your desires. By visually representing your goals and aspirations, you send a clear message to the Universe about what you want to attract into your life. As you engage in the creative process of selecting images and words that resonate with your dreams, you program your subconscious mind, call in the Knowing, and activate your RAS to filter for opportunities and resources that support your goals.

A vision board serves as a constant reminder of your intentions, keeping them at the forefront of your mind and guiding your actions toward manifesting them into reality. Through this intentional collaboration between your conscious desires, the Universe, and your brain's filtering mechanism, you empower yourself to cocreate the life you truly desire.

- Gather your materials: If using a computer, simply open a blank document where you can put images. If making a physical vision board, gather a variety of magazines and printed images, plus scissors, glue, and a piece of poster board or paper.
- Set your intentions: Before starting, reflect on your goals, dreams, and aspirations. What do you want to manifest in your life? Keep these intentions in mind as you create your vision board.

- Find visual inspiration: Search for images that represent your goals and desires. Online, Canva, Pinterest, and Google Images have high-quality pictures. Or flip through magazines and cut out images, words, and phrases that resonate.
- Create your vision board: Whether on a computer or poster board, arrange the images, words, quotes, and graphics in whatever way is visually pleasing to you. Get creative with the layout and use different colors and textures to make it visually appealing.
- Personalize your board: Add personal touches to your vision board that make it uniquely yours. Include photos of yourself, handwritten affirmations, or other meaningful elements that inspire you. Consider incorporating a theme or color scheme that resonates with your goals and preferences.
- Review and reflect: Take a step back and look at your vision board as a whole. Does it capture the essence of your dreams and aspirations? Make any adjustments or additions as needed. Spend a few moments reflecting on the images and words you've chosen. How do they make you feel? Visualize yourself living the life you desire, with all your goals and dreams coming to fruition.
- Display your vision board: Find a prominent place to display your vision board where you'll see it regularly, such as on a bulletin board, wall, or desk. Take a photo of your vision board and set it as the wallpaper on your computer or phone for daily inspiration.

Remember, creating a vision board is a fun and creative process that invites in the Knowing, so don't be afraid to let your imagination run wild and express yourself freely. Your radiance is eager to shine brightly.

CHAPTER TWENTY-TWO

Radical Commitment

*I*magine getting a haircut and stopping halfway through. Or going to school to get a professional degree, completing all the coursework, and never taking the final test. Wouldn't the results be unsatisfying? Partial commitment gets partial results.

However, when we show up and follow through with unwavering, 100 percent commitment, we get radical results. Especially when our commitment is to nurture and honor our radiance — and that is what part 5 of the POWER Method is all about. Radical commitment is an all-encompassing dedication to a way of life that centers around who we are, who we're meant to be, and what lights us up rather than focusing on external forces that disconnect us from our true essence. It involves a deep, unwavering devotion to personal growth that influences our actions, decisions, and priorities.

Radical commitment is a spiritual path to achieving great personal transformation, increased impact on others, and reaching profound levels of satisfaction and success. It's a commitment that goes beyond adhering to traditional societal standards or engaging in rebellious behavior. It embraces a lifestyle that reflects deep-seated beliefs and values, focusing on our strengths and contributions rather than on our deficiencies. It empowers us to use our talents and abilities for the greater good.

When your commitment is 100 percent, the results aren't partial — they're radical. Are you ready to give yourself that gift?

Your Character Counts

Whether we are doing something for personal satisfaction or as a professional goal doesn't matter. To reap the rewards from the desire, activity, or goal, we must have the fortitude to overcome the obstacles along the way without wavering. Energy knows the difference between 100 percent and 98 percent commitment. We can't psyche out the Universe.

How do we achieve full commitment, especially when we are entering uncharted territory? We commit to our character and the qualities of who we are and who we know we can be. Radical commitment is more about the qualities we possess rather than having a perfectly executed plan. Commitment comes from within and requires us to be active and harness our unstoppable spirit.

For example, let's pretend you are going to train for a triathlon, and you haven't even worked out in over a year. This is a pretty big challenge, yet you know that doing the triathlon is going to unlock so much related to your health, confidence, and energy. You know it'll help you unleash your potential. So you work with a trainer, a coach, or maybe an app to help set your training milestones. Some of these milestones you will absolutely crush, and others you will miss. What determines whether you keep going or not is how committed you are to the person who wants these results — yourself. Developing strong character will help you overcome the difficult trials that surface along the way.

Here are several character traits commonly seen in those who display radical commitment to their dreams, goals, and well-being:

- Persistence: A strong determination to persevere through challenges and setbacks without giving up.
- Consistency: Regular and dedicated effort toward the desired outcome, even when progress is slow or difficult.
- Focus: Maintaining unwavering attention on the goal,

avoiding distractions, and prioritizing tasks that align with the commitment.

- Passion: Genuine enthusiasm and excitement for the goal, driving motivation and fueling efforts to achieve it.
- Resilience: The ability to bounce back from failures or setbacks, learning from mistakes and using them as opportunities for growth.
- Sacrifice: Willingness to make sacrifices, such as time, energy, or resources, in pursuit of the commitment without sacrificing well-being.
- Flexibility: Being open to adapting plans and strategies as needed, while remaining steadfast to the overall goal.
- Accountability: Taking responsibility for actions and decisions related to the commitment, and holding oneself accountable for progress.
- Optimism: Maintaining a positive attitude and belief in the possibility of success, even when it feels hard or impossible.
- Wholeheartedness: Investing full energy, focus, and passion into the commitment, leaving no room for doubt or hesitation.

Which of these characteristics do you already possess? Which ones do you need to embody? What is it that you would like to see manifest into reality for yourself — a hobby, a project, a goal, a new career, a relationship? How can these characteristics help you achieve it?

The Eight Forces of Potential

When you go all-in on yourself, your goals, and your desires, you send a strong signal to the Universe that you mean business. The Universe responds with opportunities, opening doors that were closed, and giving you the ability to find a way even if the odds are stacked against you. Unwavering faith and 100 percent commitment unleash your potential. You return to your radiance and tap into Infinite Intelligence. Then life begins to unfold for you, supporting you in your pursuit of more joy, fulfillment, and connection. As you grow, new challenges will emerge as you learn how to work with and manage your potential.

There are eight primary forces of potential that will help you stay in this zone of rocking your radiance. They will help you embrace your talents, gifts, and strengths in a way that gives you deep satisfaction. They will also deepen the love you have for yourself and others. They will increase your sense of belonging and the connectedness you feel from Infinite Intelligence as well as others.

Each force is unique, and if overlooked, they can create an energetic blockage in your path to realizing your full potential. Navigating all eight forces of potential simultaneously may seem daunting. However, tackling one to three forces at a time is entirely feasible. With consistent effort and intention, you can gradually master each force, helping you develop and strengthen your character for radical commitment. All eight forces will empower you to cultivate intentionality in each aspect and ascend toward the realization of your authentic self and your fullest potential.

Here are the eight forces of potential as well as a practical way to apply them toward radical commitment.

Force 1: Profession and Passion

Clearly define your goals, aspirations, and dreams as they relate to your profession and your passions. Set specific, achievable, and meaningful objectives that align with your values and passions.

A practical and intentional framework I like to use is called SMART goals. This acronym stands for specific, measurable, achievable, relevant, and time-bound. Clear goals and dreams allow Infinite Intelligence to support our goals, bringing them into reality faster.

What is one SMART goal you can set for your dreams as it relates to your profession and/or passions?

Force 2: Mindset and Beliefs

Cultivate a positive and growth-oriented mindset. Work on aligning your beliefs and thoughts with the life you want to create, embracing optimism, resilience, and self-belief.

Your thoughts and emotions consciously and subconsciously run your world. Feed that mind with positive and self-affirming thoughts that trigger supportive radiant emotions.

Describe one thought pattern that comes from the zone of UN-potential and how you can replace it with a radiant one.

Force 3: Routines, Habits, and Actions

Intentionally design daily routines and habits that support your goals. Consistently take actions aligned with your values, as small, consistent steps lead to significant progress over time.

Action is the ultimate fear destroyer. Your routines and habits can lead you to either a lackluster life or one filled with success and satisfaction, so make sure your days mirror the outcomes you want.

What is one action you can do differently today than yesterday? Continue to do that until it becomes part of your routines and habits.

Force 4: Relationships

Be intentional about the relationships you cultivate. Surround yourself with supportive, positive, and inspiring individuals who uplift and encourage your growth.

Birds of a feather flock together, right? Hang out with the naysayers, the "I can't do it" crew, and you'll end up marinating in their negativity. You want champions by your side! Surround yourself with the cheerleaders, the visionaries, the go-getters. Seek out those folks who see your potential and raise you higher.

Who are the supportive people in your life? How can you leverage them to pull out your best qualities and strengthen your character?

Force 5: Health and Wellness

Prioritize your physical, mental, and emotional well-being. Set intentions around exercise, nutrition, self-care practices, and mental health strategies to support your overall wellness.

Your wellness and health are the key to unleashing potential. Think of it this way: You've got this toolbox of gifts, talents, and strengths waiting to be utilized, but without the energy to wield them, they'll just gather dust. Great health can fuel your unstoppable spirit.

What can you do today that would optimize your health?

Force 6: Learning and Growth

Commit to continuous learning and personal development. This helps you learn what you are capable of doing and achieving as well as strengthens the qualities of your character.

Growth is where the magic happens! You've got this incredible brain, but believe it or not, you're only tapping into a fraction of its potential. Every time you learn something new, you're better equipped for the next challenge.

Name something you could do or something new you could experience that would help you learn, grow, and discover more about who you are.

Force 7: Contribution and Service

Set intentions around giving back and making a positive impact. Identify ways to contribute to causes or communities that resonate with your values and passions, and it will help deepen your character. From volunteering your time to sharing your gifts, there are so many ways that you can make a contribution.

When you intentionally align yourself with the kind of service that ignites your soul, guess what? Doors fling wide open that you didn't even know existed. When you are in the spirit of contributing, you start serving others from your overflow of radiance, that sheer brilliance that's uniquely yours. What happens next is pure magic. You make a positive impact on the people around you.

List some ways that you can serve others in a way that feels rewarding to you.

Force 8: Spirituality and Inner Connection

Cultivate practices that deepen your spiritual connection or inner awareness. This may include meditation, mindfulness, prayer, or practices that foster a sense of inner peace and alignment.

Infinite Intelligence is supporting you and the driving force behind your most authentic and awe-inspiring goals. Intentionally embrace that power, embrace that connection, and reveal your most radiant self.

What are some practices that help you align to your peace and potential? How can these practices help you with radical commitment?

Life with Radical Commitment

Returning to and rocking your radiance takes radical commitment. And to have the unwavering dedication required, the quality of your character makes the determining factor.

You have and will go through trials and triumphs in life. Your hardships have the ability to break you down or build you up depending on your perspective and how you react. Character qualities like optimism, persistence, perseverance, resilience, passion, and consistency will help you develop an unstoppable spirit that is able to overcome even the toughest adversities. This is the truth of who you are — a radiant soul with boundless potential.

Freedom and liberation emerge as you begin to define your relationships, desires, and contributions by the values that are most meaningful to you. Life aligns to who you are rather than who you are not and the quality of your life increases exponentially.

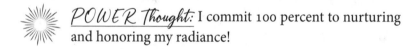 *Grab Your Gemstone:* Radical commitment is about embracing a life that mirrors your deep-seated beliefs and values, focusing on your strengths and contributions rather than deficiencies with unwavering commitment. It encourages developing character traits such as persistence, consistency, focus, passion, resilience, sacrifice, flexibility, accountability, optimism, and wholeheartedness. These qualities not only empower you to utilize your talents for the greater good but also lead to radical results in your personal and professional lives.

POWER Thought: I commit 100 percent to nurturing and honoring my radiance!

POWER Up Your Practice 22: The Eight Forces of Potential Self-Assessment

Radical commitment means knowing where you are, your starting point. This exercise is a self-assessment of your eight forces of potential. This will help you discover what forces are flowing freely, which ones might have blockages, and which ones are preventing you from rocking your radiance.

On a separate sheet of paper or in a journal, write down your rating for each of the following eight questions, using this ranking scale:

1 = Needs to be prioritized
2 = Working on it
3 = Rockin' it

- Force 1: Profession and Passion — Have you outlined your goals, aspirations, and dreams and truly defined them with specific, achievable, and meaningful objectives that align with your values and passions?
- Force 2: Mindset and Beliefs — Have you cultivated a positive and growth-oriented mindset where you are actively aligning your beliefs and thoughts with the life you want to create — embracing optimism, resilience, and self-belief?
- Force 3: Routines, Habits, and Actions — Have you intentionally designed daily routines and habits that support your goals? Do you consistently take actions aligned with your intentions, as small, consistent steps that lead you to significant progress over time?
- Force 4: Relationships — Are you intentional about the relationships you cultivate? Are you surrounding yourself with supportive, positive, and inspiring individuals who uplift and encourage your growth?
- Force 5: Health and Wellness — Do you prioritize your physical, mental, and emotional well-being? Are you setting intentions around exercise, nutrition, self-care practices, and mental health strategies to support your overall wellness?
- Force 6: Learning and Growth — Do you commit to continuous learning and personal development? Are you acquiring new skills, gaining knowledge, and expanding your horizons in areas that contribute to your growth?
- Force 7: Contribution and Service — Do you set intentions around giving back and making a positive impact? Have you identified ways to contribute to causes or communities that resonate with your values and passions?
- Force 8: Spirituality and Inner Connection — Have you

cultivated practices that deepen your spiritual connection or inner awareness? Do you include meditation, mindfulness, prayer, or practices that foster a sense of inner peace and alignment?

Reflect on your results and choose what forces you want to prioritize as you prepare to rock your radiance in the most epic ways.

CHAPTER TWENTY-THREE

Leverage Gratitude for Good

*W*hat's your favorite kind of chocolate — milk, dark, or white? Like chocolate, gratitude has three flavors: gratitude, appreciation, and thankfulness. Each is unique in their profile and yet part of the same core theme. When practiced, gratitude, appreciation, and thankfulness bring more joy and fulfillment into your life and in ways you've never known possible.

While they are similar, all three have distinctions. Here is an overview:

Gratitude: Overall, gratitude provides a deep connection to the positive gifts and opportunities life offers. Ultimately, raising your vibration and attracting more things to be grateful for helps you gain a sense of optimism for the present and the future.

Appreciation: This is a recognition of different qualities, people, situations, and events that have transpired in a way that helps you see the wonderful aspects they have contributed. Appreciation helps connect the dots of past and present in a positive way that creates a sense of inner peace.

Thankfulness: This creates positive feelings around events, experiences, and people, typically leaving you feeling pleased over an outcome or relieved that something has come to an end. It helps you stay present and enjoy more of your life.

In a nutshell, gratitude is overall love for life. Appreciation is all about recognizing the awesome qualities in something or someone — those details that make you smile. And thankfulness, well, that's responding to a specific moment or experience that's rocked your world.

Sprinkle some gratitude, appreciation, and thankfulness into each day and you will amplify your radiance. Your life will optimize in the most magnificent ways.

Discover Your Primary Question

Did you know that you have a primary question that subconsciously runs through your mind several times a day, if not more? This primary question typically is rooted in the voice of your inner critic and can keep you in your zone of UN-potential. However, if you can get to the root of the inner critic and shift it consciously to be centered in one of the three flavors of gratitude, you will reveal more of your radiance.

For example, I eventually discovered my primary question was "Am I doing enough?" This explained why I struggled with burnout and feeling disconnected all the time. I never stopped moving and doing, so it was hard to feel and to have self-awareness — there was never a pause. I lacked any of the three flavors of gratitude toward myself and the things that I did, whether for my family, my work, or myself. There was always more to be done. Have you felt like this, too? If so, your primary question might be similar.

With awareness, you can shift your primary question into a radiant frequency using gratitude, appreciation, and thankfulness. Today, my primary question is, "From a place of appreciation, how can I create more of what I love with ease and grace?" This is just an example of how intention and gratitude can be used to shift your primary question to a higher frequency where Infinite Intelligence can intercede to support and serve you. With practice and repetition, your subconscious will reprogram to align with your highest and greatest good, resulting in better outcomes.

Here are seven questions that can help you discover your current primary question:

1. What thoughts consistently occupy my mind during quiet moments?
    o   Reflecting on your thoughts during moments of silence can reveal patterns or recurring themes. For example: *I shouldn't be resting, I should be doing something.*

2. How do I react to challenges or failures?
    o   Your immediate mental response to setbacks can clue you in to the underlying beliefs about your abilities and worth. For example: *I shouldn't have done that, I know better.*

3. What do I fear others will think about me?
    o   Social fears often highlight your deepest insecurities and the questions you're subconsciously trying to answer about your value and identity. For example: *Others are going to think I'm lazy or irresponsible if I'm not proactively doing something.*

4. When do I feel the most defensive?
    o   The moments you feel the need to defend yourself can indicate areas of insecurity and the questions you might be asking yourself about your adequacy or competence. For example: *I will get called out for doing something I know I should have done but didn't.*

5. What would I need to believe about myself to feel happy and fulfilled?
    o   This question can help reveal the negative image that your subconscious might be wrestling with. For

example: *I don't believe that it's OK to rest and replenish my energy.*

6.   In what situations do I feel the least confident?

    o   Analyzing scenarios where your confidence dips can illuminate the doubts your subconscious might be entertaining. For example: *When I feel I am being micromanaged, I feel that I'm not doing anything right.*

7.   What criticism do I most fear receiving?

    o   The critiques you dread can reflect the questions you're asking about your worth, abilities, or identity. For example: *I am not doing enough at work to impact results or enough at home to keep the household running.*

If you had to sum up your subconscious thinking in one question, what do you feel your primary question is?

For example: *Am I doing enough?*

Leveraging Gratitude

Gratitude, appreciation, and thankfulness are among the highest frequency of radiant emotions. What this means is that when your thoughts, actions, and emotions stem from the three flavors of gratitude, they will positively change your outcomes and help unleash your potential for the greater good of all. You will also feel peace and grace instead of pressure and stress.

Your primary question influences your actions and decisions. Knowing that, how would a primary question rooted in gratitude, appreciation, and thankfulness change your outcomes? What do you think is possible if your subconscious mind was operating in the frequency of the three flavors of gratitude? What opportunities might open up for you?

Leverage gratitude to shift your primary question from the voice of the inner critic to the voice of your inner motivational coach. Remember, gratitude is centered in the present and the future, appreciation is centered in the past and the present, and thankfulness is centered in the present. Depending on your primary question, you can choose what flavor of gratitude you can leverage to help reshape your new primary question.

Here are seven questions that can help shift your thinking:

1. What am I grateful for in my life right now?
   - Focusing on gratitude can immediately shift your perspective from what you lack to what you possess. This question encourages a positive outlook and appreciation for the present moment. For example: *I am grateful for my health and the health of my family.*

2. What do I appreciate about my strengths, and how can I use them today?
   - Identifying and appreciating your strengths fosters a sense of competence and self-worth, shifting the focus from perceived weaknesses to inherent abilities. For example: *I appreciate my willingness to leverage my strengths and use them in a way that serves other people.*

3. What progress have I made toward my goals, and how can I be thankful for that?
   - Recognizing even small achievements with a spirit of thankfulness can boost your motivation and shift your attention from setbacks to progress and potential. For example: *I took an hour's nap, and I'm so thankful for the renewed energy I feel.*

4. Who inspires me and why?
   - Reflecting on the qualities of people you admire can help you identify values and aspirations that are

important to you, guiding your actions in a positive direction. For example: *My best friend inspires me because she maintains strong boundaries, and so she has more time and energy for what's important to her.*

5. What can I learn from this situation?
   o Viewing challenges as opportunities for learning and growth changes your mindset from victimhood to empowerment. For example: *Even though I often take action because I don't feel I do enough, I realize that I love taking action and I can do it in a more healthy and supportive way.*

6. How can I make someone's day better?
   o Shifting your focus outward to the well-being of others can enhance your sense of connection and purpose, creating a positive feedback loop that uplifts both you and those around you. For example: *I can show up with a genuine smile on my face and offer an uplifting attitude in my interactions.*

7. What steps can I take right now to nurture myself?
   o Thinking about ways to nurture yourself helps maintain a forward-focused, solution-oriented mindset, steering you away from rumination or negativity. For example: *Resting is a form of taking action that allows me to recharge.*

By regularly asking yourself these questions, you can cultivate a more positive, resilient, and proactive mindset, which helps you reframe your primary question in gratitude. This practice not only benefits your own mental and emotional well-being but also positively impacts those around you.

If you made only one new primary question, what would your new question be?

Forgiveness Creates Expansion

When we carry resentment toward others or ourselves, it takes away our space and energy, and it knocks us out of the high frequencies of the three flavors of gratitude. Forgiveness isn't about forgetting that something happened or letting someone off the hook for something they did. Forgiveness doesn't work that way. Resentment is an energy that prevents us from feeling gratitude, appreciation, and thankfulness. Forgiveness is an energy that lets them in and helps our radiance expand.

Forgiveness as it relates to gratitude is best accomplished through practice rather than contemplation. For me and my clients and students, the best method I have experienced is the Hawaiian practice called Hoʻoponopono. This beautiful word translates as "to make right" or "to correct." It's like hitting the reset button for our soul — releasing the burdens and lightening our load.

Hoʻoponopono is all about solving problems and healing through four simple phrases: "I'm sorry. Please forgive me. Thank you. I love you." These simple yet powerful words assist in making amends and inviting gratitude to expand our heart and our radiance.

This prayer works for everything — whether a troubled relationship, deep grief, work dramas, money headaches, or health issues. You name it and you can use this Hawaiian prayer for profound transformation. The coolest part is that you can resolve issues with other people without them even being present. I have healed so many unaddressed issues between me and my parents through this prayer. I have had clients resolve years of built-up resentment toward an ex-partner or a job in just a few days of practicing this. Plus, it helps you tap into the Infinite source of love and peace, replacing your pain with resolve.

Overall, the Hoʻoponopono prayer is really simple to practice, yet the more you connect to it and feel it in your body, the more transformative it is. To get the best results, sit in a quiet spot, close your eyes, and put your left hand on your heart and your right hand on your gut. This connects your mind, body, heart, and soul. Next, think of a person — even yourself — or a situation that has troubled you and bring it forward. Even if you feel this person doesn't deserve forgiveness, do it anyway. This is not about them. This is about you untangling from them and the situation. This practice works, and I encourage you to experiment with these easy steps and see what shifts for you.

Once you have named the troubling person or situation, envision them in your mind's eye and offer these words. Repeat them in this order several times:

- "I'm sorry."
- "Please forgive me."
- "Thank you."
- "I love you."

Whatever happened, whoever is at fault, for the sake of this exercise, treat your own role as neutral. The Universe knows what to do with this prayer, and the act of this practice untangles your energy, allowing more space to feel gratitude, appreciation, and thankfulness for yourself and your life. The gifts that the three flavors of gratitude offer are more space, energy, and time for the things that matter to you most. Then the Universe multiplies their impact in your favor, unleashing more of your light into the world.

Grab Your Gemstone: By integrating gratitude, appreciation, and thankfulness into your daily mindset and questioning, you create a path toward more fulfilling outcomes and a deeper connection with yourself and the Universe. This approach not only alters your personal frequency to attract more positivity but also encourages a more intentional, joyous, and expansive living, showcasing gratitude as a powerful tool for your personal transformation.

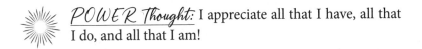

POWER Thought: I appreciate all that I have, all that I do, and all that I am!

POWER Up Your Practice 23: Ho'oponopono for Advanced Healing

For more advanced healing, use the Ho'oponopono prayer toward yourself as the recipient of the prayer on behalf of someone who has hurt you. This is the part of the practice that has helped hundreds of people I have worked with, allowing them to move forward from the pain and sorrow they have carried around for decades.

Sadly, sometimes we need an apology from someone who will never give it. That might be due to stubbornness or the fact that they are not physically on earth anymore. There is a saying: It's not "what's wrong with you," it's "who's wrong with you." The mind is powerful, and our imagination can release us from our own internal purgatory. This practice allows you to take ownership and clear the space of pain that otherwise could stick with you for a lifetime.

Believe it or not, these steps clear the slate and bring on the reconciliation. Your inner peace gets restored, and it creates room for your great expansion.

- Imagine the situation that bothers you and the person involved. Now envision them speaking these words to you: "I'm sorry." Just let the words wash over you.
- Envision the person saying to you with kindness and compassion: "Please forgive me." See them owning up to the problem and asking for forgiveness.
- Next, hear them say, "Thank you." This indicates their appreciation for being given the chance to forgive.
- Last, imagine them saying, "I love you." Imagine them sending you unconditional love for bearing a cross that was never your burden. As with the regular Ho'oponopono practice, repeat this sequence as many times as needed until you feel the release.

The next time life gets messy, and you are carrying a burden that is not yours to carry, remember these four magical phrases. They will help you get things back on track and open up room for appreciation. You only get to live this life once. Imagine living the very best, most epic life that you can — free from the shackles of your past so you can soar into the limitless possibilities of your future.

CHAPTER TWENTY-FOUR

The Beautiful Unfolding

*A*lignment with the truth of who you are is the most incredible gift you can give yourself, for it results in the beautiful unfolding of a life filled with passion, potential, and purpose. Applying everything you have learned up to this point — from the concepts to the practical how-tos to the exercises — aligns your human self with your Infinite soul. As a result, life starts working for you rather than against you.

Your life is meant to be beautiful and flowing, filled with harmony and ease. That doesn't always mean that life is going to be easy, but your journey shouldn't feel burdensome. The practices in this book may take weeks, months, and even years to become integrated into your life and that is OK. Returning to your radiance takes radical commitment, which means a lifetime of dedication to yourself and your personal growth.

As a reward for all your hard work and dedication, you won't have to power through life with the same intensity, leading to disconnection and burnout. Instead, you will be in harmony with your life, trusting yourself and the Universe to reveal what's next. The beautiful unfolding is the gift the Universe presents as a result of alignment with your true essence and all that you were born to be.

Harmonious Alignment

Have you ever taken a break from something or given yourself space from a task, only to come back to it and easily resolve it? Has life ever forced you to take a break or change your direction, and to your surprise, it ended up being a good thing? Sometimes we can push and try so hard that we knock ourselves out of alignment, making it difficult for the Universe to support us. Then somehow the pause button gets hit, either by choice or life's unpredictable force, and much to our surprise things get rearranged into working order. This is what happened to Jackie.

Jackie was a senior leader at a Fortune 500 company and worked fifty-hour weeks regularly. She was the driving force behind much of her department's success. However, on the inside, Jackie was massively out of alignment with the truth of who she was. Her identity was tied to her role as a senior leader for her organization, and then she was laid off. This was crushing to Jackie, and she felt like everything she knew and stood for had been taken from her.

Forced to reevaluate her life, Jackie reflected on other areas of her life within the eight forces of potential. In doing so she realized that she had only developed two or three of them, and their development was centered around her job. A few weeks after her layoff, Jackie also found out she was diagnosed with stage one breast cancer.

On the surface, Jackie felt like her life was falling apart, and in some respects it was. However, Jackie had an unstoppable spirit and strong character, qualities that she could redirect toward beating cancer and redefining the next phase of her career. Rather than hyperfocusing on what was wrong, with the help of guidance from myself and a handful of other practitioners, Jackie began to focus on what was right in her life and what brought her joy.

This was counterintuitive for Jackie. But she was desperate to heal and to love her life again, so she radically committed to discovering herself and learning what it looked like to prioritize her health and well-being. She began feeling her way into what served her and what did not by checking in with herself to see if she felt harmony or disharmony with the actions and choices she was making. The more she made choices that were in harmony with herself, the more life aligned to her with ease and grace. She didn't have to try so hard.

With more ease and grace by her side, it preserved the energy for healing, and she was able to beat cancer. Learning what harmony felt like within her body and her spirit, she was able to explore and navigate the eight forces of potential until she knew what she valued and what was meaningful to her. She emerged back in the workforce as a vice president at another Fortune 500 company that valued its people. This allowed Jackie the space to nurture herself as well as the relationships that matter most to her.

Finally, Jackie reached a point in her life where her human self and her soul were in harmonious alignment and life began to unfold in the most beautiful and unexpected ways. Today, Jackie has published two books, is an advocate and mentor for women with breast cancer, works full-time with a flexible schedule so she can do more of what she loves, leads a team of self-reliant leaders that are dedicated to personal growth and the growth of the company, and has received several awards for the contributions she has made. Jackie didn't plan any of this. Each opportunity unfolded in front of her as she committed to being in harmonious alignment with herself. Most importantly, this beautiful unfolding led to Jackie feeling extreme amounts of joy, appreciation, and contribution to life, as well as deep satisfaction about her quality of life.

Wouldn't it be nice not to try so hard to make things happen? Wouldn't it be nice to navigate life's adversities with more ease and grace? Wouldn't it be nice to feel joy and deep satisfaction? This is all available to you when you are in flow with yourself and the Universe.

Getting into a Flow State

A flow state with the Universe is a deeply harmonious and synchronized state where our actions and intentions align perfectly with the natural order of the Universe's energy. In this state, our effort seems minimal, and actions and outcomes unfold easily and successfully, creating a sense of unity and connectedness with everything. It's a state of being where our intuition is heightened, and there's a profound sense of being part of a larger, guiding flow of energy, leading to peak experiences and optimal performance.

How do you know if you are in harmonious alignment and in a flow state? There are ways you can check in with yourself to validate whether you are or not. One way is with the Self & Soul Check-In Technique, below. This will help you tap into yourself and the Universe to feel your answers so you can stay in a flow state.

Self & Soul Check-In Technique

To start, close your eyes, roll your shoulders back, and release any tension in your face. Take a deep breath in and out through your nose. Continue long deep breathing with eyes closed through the duration of this practice. Place your left hand on your heart and your right hand on your gut.

- After another deep inhale and exhale, set your intention and ask your question. For example: *I call on my higher self to help me stay in alignment with my truth. Does this person, situation, or decision serve my highest and greatest good?*
- Keep breathing until you feel either harmony or disharmony within:
  - Feelings of harmony might be peace, joy, excitement, goose bumps, and butterflies.
  - Feelings of disharmony might be uncertainty, doubt, nausea, shallow breathing, and concern.
- When you are done, write down what you felt. Did you have feelings of harmony or disharmony? Were there any

thoughts or awareness that entered your consciousness? If
so, what were they?

- Make your decisions based on feelings of harmony. If you
feel disharmony, then keep checking in until you find the
harmonious answer.

When your primary state is in harmony with yourself and
your surroundings, it puts you in a flow state with the Universe.
Your radiance takes the lead, and you once again are connected to
life on a bigger and grander scale. Your body heals and optimizes,
your potential is unleashed, and miracles present themselves.

Embrace Your Magic

Did you know that you truly are magical in your own unique way?
With over twenty thousand genes in the human genome plus epi-
genetic and environmental factors, it's impossible for two people
to be the same. Even identical twins have differences. There are
ideas, concepts, and art that only you can create. So it's important
to embrace your magic and use it to cocreate with the Universe.
This adds another layer to the beautiful unfolding that is available
to you when you are in your radiance.

Sometimes we struggle with perfectionism so much that it
stops us from starting something new. Or since others are already
doing what we want to do, we decide we can't. The good news is
Infinite Intelligence doesn't work that way. The Universe encourages us to bring our uniqueness forward. Whether you consider
yourself an artist or not, you are in fact the artist of your life. And
just like an artist, you have a magical expression inside that wants
to be revealed and shared with others.

Embracing your magic means saying yes to ideas and passions
as they come alive inside. The goal of creating and sharing your
magic with the world is not about what you achieve, such as becoming famous or a world champion — although you could. The

goal is to take joy in your authentic self-expression, whatever that may be.

When you embrace your magic and allow it to create through you, the beautiful unfolding supports you and shows you what's next, one courageous step at a time. Let's face it, breaking the societal mold and allowing your radiance to shine takes guts. The payoff is worth it because the Universe reveals more about your path and your purpose each time you bravely take action to express your truth. It's not something you have to figure out ahead of time. Your magic will guide you. You'll create a ripple effect of positivity that inspires others and contributes to the greater good.

Here are ten ways you can embrace and share your magic:

1. Pursue your passions: Dedicate time to activities and pursuits that light you up inside, whether it's art, music, writing, or any other form of creative expression.

2. Speak your truth: Communicate your thoughts, beliefs, and feelings openly and honestly in conversations, both in personal and professional settings.

3. Live by your values: Make decisions based on your personal values and beliefs, not just societal expectations or pressures. This integrity in action is a powerful form of self-expression.

4. Share your story: Every person's life experience is unique. Sharing your journey, the challenges you've faced, and how you've overcome them can inspire and encourage others.

5. Embrace your style: Let your personal style reflect who you are. Whether through fashion, art, or lifestyle, how you present yourself to the world can be a celebration of your individuality.

6. Teach and mentor: Use your knowledge, skills, and experiences to teach or mentor others. Sharing your expertise in a way that resonates with your core beliefs can be incredibly fulfilling.

7. Volunteer for causes you believe in: Giving your time

and energy to causes that matter to you is a meaningful way to contribute your unique gifts to the world.

8. Create and innovate: Don't be afraid to try new things and innovate in your field of interest or work. Original ideas and approaches can pave the way for new discoveries and inspire others.

9. Listen to your intuition: Your intuition is a powerful guide. Making choices that feel right to you, even when they defy logic, can lead to a fulfilling and authentic life path.

10. Practice self-reflection: Regularly spend time reflecting on your life, goals, and the person you're becoming. This self-awareness can guide you in making choices that truly reflect your inner self.

By embracing these approaches, you can share your uniqueness and magic with the world in ways that not only are authentic but enrich the lives of others. Each time you boldly share your truth, the Universe unfolds in organic and beautiful ways that reveal a little bit more of what's next for you, without you trying to control the how. This results in a harmonious alignment with your true self and more feelings of joy, freedom, and fulfillment.

Grab Your Gemstone: Aligning with your true self is the ultimate gift that leads to a life brimming with passion, potential, and purpose. By integrating the lessons learned, from personal growth concepts to practical exercises, you can synchronize your human experience with your infinite soul, making life work for you rather than against you. This allows you to embrace and share your inner magic in a way that fulfills you and uplifts others.

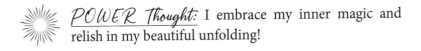

POWER Thought: I embrace my inner magic and relish in my beautiful unfolding!

POWER UP Your Practice 24: The Joyful Surrender Dance

There is an art to allowing the Universe to beautifully unfold in your favor, which includes letting go of control. Control and perfectionism are hard for a lot of people, so if you struggle with them, too, you are not alone. Controlling outcomes gets in the way of beautiful unfolding, so learning to joyfully surrender into this state of grace is key to the best possible outcomes.

This means we set goals, take action, and, well, leave the outcome to Infinite Intelligence, knowing that it will deliver something far better than we could on our own. To help get in the flow of a joyful surrender, a fun and easy practice is to dance.

Pick a song that makes you want to move and groove and dance like no one is watching. Close your eyes and allow your body to move — no scripts, no specific dance moves. Just move to the beat of the music, invite your soul in, and joyfully surrender to movement. This helps you loosen control, and fun is an invitation to the Universe to intercede and cocreate with you. Don't overthink it, just do it — and don't forget to smile!

CHAPTER TWENTY-FIVE

Love, Leadership, and Legacy

*H*ave you ever stopped to consider the legacy you are leaving behind? Regardless of what stage of life you are in and what you do for a living, if you transitioned out of this world tomorrow, what do you think people would say about you? Would you take pride in their remarks, or would their comments make you cringe? Have you expressed everything you came here to express — from your abilities to the qualities of your character to your capacity to love? Do you feel you have made a positive impact, whether it be big or small?

These questions are important to consider, and oftentimes we don't think about them until late in life. As part of returning to radiance, answer these questions now to your satisfaction so that when your time of transition comes, you are filled with love and acceptance for a life well lived.

When you live in a radiant state, it doesn't mean life is perfect. Life will still offer adversities and obstacles, but you will approach them from your whole self rather than your disconnected self. And when you return to radiance, not only do you feel a difference in your quality of life, but this radiates out to others. As a result, love, leadership, and legacy become part of your spirit, and you become an uplifting source for other people by showing them what's possible.

In Alcoholics Anonymous, it's said that, on average, each person impacts a minimum of six lives on a day-to-day basis. Imagine if you uplifted a minimum of six people, not because you were trying to, but just because you were being you. Now imagine that you positively impacted more than six people. How does that ripple effect make you feel? This ripple is what happens when you live in a radiant state. So are you ready to leave behind a legacy to be proud of?

Love

Love is among the strongest, if not the strongest, and highest emotions we possess. Love unites. Love heals. Love uplifts. Love expands past our romantic and close relationships and extends to all. Love can generate miracles. Love is the full expression of Infinite Intelligence through us. So let's talk about love and why it's such a big deal.

Love is the ultimate glue, bringing folks together, and making us feel connected and like we belong. It strengthens relationships and builds communities. Love's got this magic touch that helps us walk in someone else's shoes and see them through compassionate eyes. It helps us be more kind, makes us hug a bit tighter, and become more supportive and caring.

Love isn't just an emotional healer; it's got physical healing powers, too. Love calms our nerves, soothes our pain, and keeps our mental and physical health in check. It guides us to nurture relationships, lend a helping hand, or make a positive dent in the Universe. Here's the positive thing about love — love doesn't care about what separates us or the latest trends. It's timeless, ageless, and celebrated worldwide for its incredible impact on humanity.

In a nutshell, love's like this ultimate superhero fueling connections, boosting empathy, patching us up, and making life a heck of a lot more awesome. Your radiance levels up love and keeps your world spinning with joy and meaning. Love becomes the gift you give yourself and others when you stay radically committed to your personal growth.

When your love starts to feel big and you can be supportive

of others in a way that does not drain you, here are some ideas to share your big love in uplifting ways:

- Listen actively: Give others your full attention when they speak, showing genuine interest in their thoughts and feelings without judgment.
- Offer encouragement: Be a cheerleader, especially during challenging times. Remind others of their strengths and past successes.
- Be present: Simply being there for someone can be incredibly comforting. Show up for important events or during tough times.
- Express appreciation: Regularly tell and show people how much you appreciate them and their presence in your life.
- Encourage self-care: Remind others to take care of themselves and support them in doing activities that promote their well-being.
- Offer resources: If people face challenges, help them to find resources or solutions, whether by recommending a book, sharing a helpful article, or finding a professional to talk to.
- Celebrate successes: Be genuinely happy for someone's achievements and celebrate with them, no matter how small the victory may seem.

By incorporating these practices into your interactions, you can build stronger, more meaningful connections and create a supportive, loving environment for others.

Leadership

When you rock your radiance, you give others permission to do the same. You become a leader the moment you choose to return to your radiance and share your true self with the world. Through your actions, you show that it's more important to defy societal expectations and live in the truth of who you are than it is to conform and live disconnected and burned out.

For example, let's pretend you decide to try stand-up comedy just because you have always wanted to do it. You don't care about earning a living or becoming famous. You truly only want to learn and enjoy the craft. As a result, when your friends and family come out to support you at open-mic nights, they see you glowing in your radiance and having fun. That inspires some of them to pursue their passions, and as they catch the radiant glow, they inspire even more people to find their joy, too.

Without meaning to or knowing it, just by you doing you, you are leading people. Your joy inspires others to seek theirs. Good leaders are like cheerleaders for the soul. Except you don't wave pom-poms. You give permission and create spaces for everyone to shine, grow, and be their awesome unique selves.

Whether it's in the boardroom, in a comedy club, or in the neighborhood, leaders are the architects of change, leaving behind a legacy that inspires others to create positive change in their lives. This is what is in store for you — leading through influence as you become the change you want to see in the world.

Leadership is more than a virtue; it lights up the path for others. It guides, inspires, and empowers, making everyone's journey a heck of a lot more fabulous. This is what happens when we decide to step up, set new standards, and be 100 percent ourselves.

Leading and influencing others through action involves embodying the qualities and behaviors you wish to inspire in those around you. Here are several ways to do this:

- Exemplify integrity: Demonstrate honesty and consistency in your words and actions. Integrity builds trust.
- Practice empathy: Show genuine concern for others' feelings and perspectives. Empathy fosters a supportive environment where everyone feels valued.
- Communicate effectively: Be clear, open, and respectful

in your communication. Listen actively and acknowledge others' ideas, which encourages collaboration.

- Be accountable: Take responsibility for your actions and their outcomes. Owning your mistakes and learning from them sets a powerful example for others.
- Demonstrate resilience: Face challenges with a positive attitude and a willingness to persevere. Your resilience can inspire others to navigate difficulties with grace.
- Encourage growth: Invest in your own continuous learning and development, and encourage others to do the same. Share resources, knowledge, and opportunities to grow.
- Show appreciation: Regularly acknowledge and appreciate the efforts and contributions of others. Recognition can boost someone's morale and motivate them to be their best.

By embodying these actions and qualities, you can effectively lead others through inspiration and influence, fostering a mindset of growth and potential.

Legacy

What does it mean to leave behind a legacy? It means impacting people in ways that persist longer than we do. To be in a position where we leave a legacy behind means that we are embodying our radiant gifts and qualities. We aren't trying to be radiant; we just are. This is why this journey is a *return* to radiance. There is nothing you have to do or create to become radiant. You were born radiant. It's already yours to embrace and share.

My brother passed away in a tragic accident at the age of forty-three, leaving behind a wife and three kids. For much of his adult life, he struggled with alcoholism and spent time in and out of recovery programs trying his best to maintain sobriety.

My brother's passing was different from my mom's and my dad's. While my mom and dad became disconnected from their radiance and ended up depressed and dis-eased, my brother had returned to his.

At the time of his passing, he was sober. More important than that, he had made amends for wrongs that impacted his wife, his kids, me, and the Universe. He embodied love, leadership, and legacy in his day-to-day actions and his conversations. You could see and feel his inner light radiating outward. During his celebration of life and in the wake of the announcement of his passing, I received countless messages from people saying that my brother had changed their lives. He did this through conversations that motivated and empowered others, through acts of kindness that helped someone in their sobriety journey, and by using his connections to help people get a job.

At forty-three, my brother had returned to his radiance. Even though his passing was painful, it was also filled with so much beauty, and so much love surrounded him and the people he interacted with. Although my brother accomplished many things, people were most impacted by who he was and the qualities he embodied. He left behind a legacy to be proud of.

This is an example of what returning to your radiance can mean. It improves your ability to love, lead, and make an impact. Leaving behind your own legacy of impact involves intentional actions and meaningful conversations that positively influence others and the world.

Here are several ways to create a lasting legacy:

- Live your values: Consistently act in alignment with your core values. When your life reflects your beliefs, you inspire others to consider and live by their own values.
- Mentor and teach: Share your knowledge, skills, and experiences with others. Mentoring or teaching can change lives by empowering individuals to reach their full potential.

- Lead by example: Be the change you wish to see in the world. Your actions can serve as a powerful model for personal and professional growth, encouraging others to do the same.
- Foster community: Build and nurture communities that support growth, learning, and mutual support. Strong communities can amplify your impact well beyond individual efforts.
- Advocate for change: Stand up for causes you believe in and use your voice to advocate for positive change. Even small efforts can lead to significant shifts over time.
- Be generous: Share your time, resources, and compassion generously. Acts of kindness and generosity often have a ripple effect, spreading far wider than you might imagine.
- Engage in meaningful conversations: Seek out and engage in conversations that challenge, inspire, and motivate. Meaningful dialogue can spark ideas, shift perspectives, and drive action.

By integrating these actions and approaches into your life, you can leave behind a legacy of impact that continues to inspire and benefit others long into the future.

Grab Your Gemstone: A life lived in radiance — a state where you are fully connected to and expressive of your true self — transforms how challenges are faced, radiates positivity to others, and fundamentally changes the quality of your life and of those around you. Love is a powerful, unifying force that heals and uplifts, leadership sets a positive example for others, and both create a legacy that leaves a lasting positive impact.

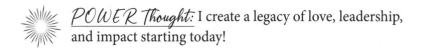

POWER Thought: I create a legacy of love, leadership, and impact starting today!

POWER Up Your Practice 25: Sat Nam

Sat Nam is a mantra that is commonly used in Kundalini yoga. *Sat Nam* means "truth is my identity" or "truth is my name." By chanting Sat Nam, we affirm our true essence and connect it with the Universal truth.

Sat Nam is also a seed mantra, a sound that activates the energy centers — the chakras in the body. By repeating it, you align your vibration with the frequency of truth and harmony. Sat Nam can be used as a greeting, a farewell, or a way of expressing gratitude.

Sat Nam is also a meditation technique. It helps focus the mind and calm the emotions. Sat Nam is a powerful mantra that can help you discover your life's purpose and live in your truth.

Practicing Sat Nam

The technique is very simple: On your inhale, think or say, "Sat," and on your exhale, think or say, "Nam." I encourage you to use Sat Nam during transition times to reset yourself. For example, when you are going from one meeting to another, when you return home after your workday, and when you wake up but before getting out of bed, briefly close your eyes and chant the mantra Sat Nam to the cadence of long and relaxing deep breaths.

Another approach, if you want more intentionality and purpose with this powerful mantra, is to find your pulse and say, "Sat Nam," either silently or out loud along with your heartbeat. This syncs and connects your true infinite identity with your humanness — unifying you in your truth and your destiny.

This practice will help you return to radiance again and again.

Conclusion

*Y*ou are the only person in the entire world with your unique strengths, talents, gifts, and experiences. Now is the time to go deeper into yourself so that you can become one with your greatness. Inside you is the ability to illuminate yourself and the world around you. Ignite your soul, unleash your potential, and soar into success. Why? Because you deserve to feel the glory of your radiance manifested in this lifetime.

The teachings in this book have the power to transform you, your dreams, your teams, your business, and your life in the most profound and magical ways. The POWER Method can cultivate extreme levels of fulfillment, joy, success, and deep meaning. Nurturing your potential isn't some simple journey you wrap up in a day. No shortcuts, no magic wands — it takes radical commitment. It's an inside job that only you can accomplish.

Your soul craves passion, curiosity, and the thrill of discovery. Your radiance isn't just a vibe; it's something you were born to express. Lots of folks have forgotten what sets their soul on fire. I hope that this book awakens the fire inside you — your burning and yearning for more. My parents knew what their radiance felt like. When they conformed to what they thought they were supposed to be and do, tragically, their light burned out. But that's their story, not yours. Today, you get to choose your radiance in the same way my brother chose his.

Welcome to a new world where you go first and show others the way. When you let your brilliance shine, you become the button pusher, the trailblazer, and the leader of a new way. You're not alone in this journey. We're in this together. We will set new standards, break the norms, and oh, will we sparkle!

The transformative power of a return to radiance is YOU. Self-discovery will lead you to pursue your destiny. Step by step your potential will be unleashed in magical ways because infinite possibilities exist. Take one last lesson from guitar Bob — step into the spotlight of your life with so much confidence that it leaves others questioning whether you can pull it off. Go deeper and pull forward your radiance as you bring the audience of your life into an awe-inspiring standing ovation. Never stop shining.

Sat Nam, fierce one.

Acknowledgments

Writing a book and having the courage to share your radiance with the world requires a ton of support. It's a team thing much more than I ever imagined before I started writing. I have to thank my family first — my husband, Jermey, for always being my rock. My daughter, Tyler, and my son, Braydon, thanks for supporting me through this process with love and a listening ear when I needed to bounce concepts off somebody. To my other kiddos, Clayton and Hailey, thank you for your love and support. To all my extended family and best friends, thank you for believing in me.

To my business partner, Lynae Looney, you are a rock star. Thank you for running the business, cheering me on, and being committed to making a difference in the world with our work. To my coaches Allison Walsh, Siri Lindley, and Nancy Levin, thank you for your unwavering support and guidance during the writing process and my overall evolution of the past few years. To the powerhouse team at Brand Builders Group: Kristen Hartnagel, Elle Petrillo, and Jeremy Weber for helping me and all of Team Becca get this message out into the world. To everyone on Team Becca, thank you for all you do!

To my writing coach, Sarah Bossenbroek, I am grateful for your help. We are two books in and counting! To Georgia Hughes, my editor, and the team at New World Library, thank you for believing in the message of this book and in me. Together, we will help more people return to the truth of who they are and shine bright in their radiance.

To the Universe, thank you for leading me and guiding me in the direction of my highest potential. Through a series of synchronicities I met Bill Philipps and Kim Corbin, also from New World Library. This was the connection that brought this book into existence, and for that I'm beyond grateful.

To my brother, Patrick, thank you for reinforcing the importance of returning to your radiance. Your soul continues to ignite the light in others because you found the light in yourself. May your legacy live on through your wife, your children, those you've touched, and through my writing.

And to you, fierce one, for having the guts and courage to break the mold, ignite what sets your soul on fire, and unleash your potential. You are the light the world needs now more than ever.

Notes

Chapter 1: Break Up with Burnout

p. 11   *According to a 2022 survey of eight thousand people conducted*: Becca Powers, *The Workplace Burnout Workbook: Learn How to Understand, Identify, and Breakup with Burnout* (Lake Worth, FL: Anxious Lotus Publications, 2023).

Chapter 2: The BS That Holds You Back

p. 23   *Did you know that a whopping 80 percent of the residue*: Bessel van der Kolk, *The Body Keeps the Score* (New York: Penguin Books, 2014).

Chapter 3: Power Up Your Choices

p. 31   *According to a 2023 survey published by the American*: American Psychological Association, "2023 Work in America Survey: Workplaces as Engines of Psychological Health and Well-Being," accessed February 19, 2024, https://www.apa.org/pubs/reports/work-in-america/2023-work place-health-well-being.

p. 33   *"When the energy of the soul is recognized, acknowledged"*: Gary Zukav, *The Seat of the Soul* (New York: Simon & Schuster, 1989/2014), 16.

Chapter 5: Permission to Have Super Big Dreamy Goals

p. 44   *According to research at Scranton University, only 8 percent*: Marcel Schwantes, "Science Says 92 Percent of People Don't Achieve Their Goals. Here's How the Other 8 Percent Do," *Inc.*, July 26, 2016, https://www.inc.com/marcel-schwantes/science-says-92-percent-of-people-dont-achieve-goals-heres-how-the-other-8-perce.html.

p. 51   *To put this in perspective, in terms of what people fear*: Soocial, "22 Fear of Failure Statistics to Change the Way You Think (2024)," accessed February 19, 2024, https://www.soocial.com/fear-of-failure-statistics.

Chapter 7: Align with Your Values

p. 67   *In a study on emotional intelligence and self-awareness*: Tasha Eurich, "What Self-Awareness Really Is (and How to Cultivate It)," *Harvard Business Review*, January 4, 2018, https://hbr.org/2018/01/what-self-awareness -really-is-and-how-to-cultivate-it.

Chapter 8: Shine Brighter Than Your Doubts

p. 75   *According to a survey by the social network Linkagoal*: Peg Moline, "We're Far More Afraid of Failure Than Ghosts: Here's How to Stare It Down," *Los Angeles Times*, October 31, 2015, https://www.latimes.com/health/la -he-scared-20151031-story.html.

Chapter 14: Unlock Abundance

p. 136   *According to Makewish.org, here are the top wishes*: "Exploring the Top 20 Wishes People Make: Unveiling Dreams and Aspirations," Makewish.org, accessed April 22, 2024, https://www.makewish.org/exploring-the-top-20 -wishes-people-make-unveiling-dreams-and-aspirations.

Chapter 16: The Yoga of Self-Awareness

p. 155   *According to a 2024 Pew Research Center study, 64 percent*: Pew Research Center, "Spirituality Among Americans: 3. Spiritual Practices," December 7, 2023, https://www.pewresearch.org/religion/2023/12/07/spiritual-practices.

About the Author

ℬ ecca Powers is a Fortune 500 high-tech sales executive, keynote speaker, founder and CEO of Powers Peak Potential, and author of *Harness Your Inner CEO*. She has worked with industry giants Cisco, Dell, Royal Caribbean International, and Office Depot. With an impressive record of leading large teams and hitting $500 million in annual revenue, Powers has earned the coveted President's Club award seven times. She is a go-to interview subject for *Newsweek*, Thrive Global, *Daily Mail*, and *Authority Magazine*, as well as dozens of podcasts. A certified Kundalini yoga teacher and Reiki master, she lives in Florida.

BeccaPowers.com